THE

BUDDHIST TRIPITAKA

AS IT IS KNOWN IN

CHINA AND JAPAN

THE

BUDDHIST TRIPITAKA

AS IT IS KNOWN IN

CHINA AND JAPAN.

A Catalogue And Compendious Report.

BY

SAMUEL BEAL

GYAN

Published by

Gyan Publishing House
5, Ansari Road
Daryaganj, New Delhi-110002
Phone: 011-47034999, 9811692060
E-mail: books@gyanbooks.com

Distribution Network
gyanbooks.com
India, USA, Canada, UK, Australia

ISBN: 978-93-6208-354-8 (HB)
First Published, 1876

2nd Impression 2024

Printed at: Gyan Press, Delhi.

THE BUDDHIST TRIPITAKA AS IT IS KNOWN IN CHINA AND JAPAN
Author: SAMUEL BEAL

大明三藏聖教

THE

BUDDHIST TRIPITAKA

AS IT IS KNOWN IN

CHINA AND JAPAN

A Catalogue and Compendious Report.

BY

SAMUEL BEAL,

MEMBER OF THE ROYAL ASIATIC SOCIETY.

PRINTED FOR THE INDIA OFFICE

BY

CLARKE & SON,

BOOKSELLERS AND STATIONERS TO HER MAJESTY, FORE STREET, DEVONPORT.

1876.

"*That Mr. Beal be requested to prepare a compendious Report of the Buddhist Tripitaka—to be ready in six months.*"

Extract from an Order of the Secretary of State in Council,
India Office, December 14th, 1875.

To Dr. R. ROST,

Librarian, the India Office, London.

Devonport, June 19th, 1876.

SIR,

I have the honor of submitting for your approval the following Catalogue and brief Report of the Books comprised in the Buddhist Tripitaka, lately sent to this country from Japan.

It will be evident from a glance at the number of Books that a full Report of their contents could not be prepared within the time allowed me for completing this Catalogue.

Nevertheless, sufficient has been done, I believe, to show the peculiar value of this collection. Embracing, as it does, the writings of the early and late, or, Southern and Northern, Schools of Buddhism, it will be seen that we have materials at hand for a complete history of that religion in all its developments.

But there are also a great number of volumes devoted to the early writings of the Buddhist Schools of China, particularly that of Tien-tai, and the Southern Contemplative (Tsung) School. And no history of Buddhism can be complete unless it reaches to these Schools, as they undoubtedly embrace within them many millions of followers, and in old time filled a still more important place in the religious history of China and Japan, the Tien-tai School being known in this latter country as Ten-dai.

The important Books relating to the Buddhist Patriarchs (Case LXXIX.) deserve particular notice, as the history of the Buddhist succession is mixed up with the secular history of India, and will probably, when thoroughly examined, throw some light on contemporaneous events, and perhaps dynastic changes, in that country.

The value of the Records of the 'Chinese Pilgrims' who visited India, and the account of whose travels is contained in this collection, is too well understood to need any remark. I regret that none of the Books alluded to by M. Stas. Julien in his introduction to the "Life of Hiouen Thsang," and which he thought might be found in Japan, are contained in this collection; but there is still some hope that they may be discovered in a separate form in some of the remote monasteries of that country, or more probably in China itself.

I cannot conclude this letter without alluding to the generosity of the Japanese Government in presenting this large and most important body of Books to the Library of the India Office, in honourable fulfilment of a promise made by his Excellency IWAKURA TOMOMI, who, when in this country, had undertaken, at your own and my solicitation, to procure them for the advantage of those interested in their contents. And although the number of students in this country who can consult their pages is at present but a small one, yet I cannot doubt that the importance of the subject, and the field for original research thus opened up, will, ere long, induce some of our younger scholars to acquire a knowledge of the Chinese-Buddhistic language, sufficient at least to render these Books serviceable in the study of this branch of the Religious History of the world.

I am, Sir,

Your obedient Servant,

SAMUEL BEAL.

P.S.—I regret that I have been unable to obtain Chinese type for the purpose of illustration. I must also explain that I could not find any type with the usual accents and diacritical points in this place.

Succession of dynasties in China [from the time of the Introduction of Buddhism, to the Ming dynasty.]

Ming-te, of the Eastern Han dynasty	58 A.D
The Wei and Wu Periods	168—190 „
The After* Han dynasty	221—223 „
The Western Tsin dynasty	265—313 „
The Eastern Tsin	317—419 „
The Yaou-Tsin Period	*circ.* 406 „
The Northern Sung, or the Northern Wei	420—477 „
The Tse dynasty, or the Seaou-Tse	479—501 „
The Liang dynasty	502—555 „
The Chin dynasty	557—583 „
The Tsui dynasty	589—619 „
The Tang dynasty	620—904 „
Minor dynasties	907—960 „
The Sung dynasty (including the *Southern* Sung)	960—1278 „
The Yuen dynasty	1280—1333 „
The Ming dynasty, to the Emperor Wan-lieh	1368—1573 „

* In the Hae-kwo-tu-chi, there is no distinction made between the Eastern Han and the After Han dynas

ERRATA.

In the early pages of the Catalogue, *e.gr.*, p. 5, l. 17, the Proper name ***Dharmagupta*** should *Dharmaraksha*.

P. 9, l. 8., for ***Aryakasagaribha*** read ***Aryakasagarbha.***

P. 15, l. 1, for ***Min*** read ***Miu or Miau.***

Do., l. 5, for *Survana* read *Suvarna.*

P. 27, l. 14, for *Vasubhandou* read *Vasubandhu.*

P. 33, l. 7, for *hing* read *king.*

P. 36, l. 11, for 18 ***Vaggas*** read 81 ***do.***

P. 38, l. 28, for ***Upasikwa*** read ***Upasikawa.***

P. 39, l. 11, for ***Sukya*** read ***Sakya.***

P. 53, l. 25, for XXXVI. read XXXIV.

P. 63, last line, for *Tautra* read *Tantra.*

P. 67, l. 14, for *Pitakanaigraha* read *Pitakanigraha.*

P. 73, l. 2, for ***Pratismoksha*** read ***Pratimoksha.***

P. 75, l. 12, read ***Sastra.***

P. 85, l. 3, for ***Asvagosha*** read ***Asvaghosha.***

P. 87, l. 15, for ***do.*** read ***do.***

Do., l. 21, for ***Tautra*** read ***Tantra.***

Do. l. 23, omit the circumflex over ***a*** in ***Dhammapadavâdana.***

P. 88, l. 19, omit the circumflex over ***a*** in ***Asokavâdana.***

THE Buddhist TRIPITAKA, Printed in Chinese Characters, with Japanese Notations in the KATAGANA Characters, lately presented by the Japanese Government to the Library of the India Office.

A CATALOGUE AND COMPENDIOUS REPORT.

This Copy of the Buddhist TRIPITAKA is that commonly known in China as the Northern Collection, because it was made by order of the Emperor Wan-lieh, towards the end of the Sixteenth Century, after the capital had been changed from Nanking (Southern Capital), to Peking (Northern Capital).

It was re-produced in Japan in the 6th year of the period *(Nengo)* IM-PO, A.D. 1679, and afterwards issued, with an Imperial Preface, in the period TEN-WA, A.D. 1681, to A.D. 1683.

As first received at the Library of the India Office, the collection was contained in seven large boxes, carefully packed in lead, with padding of dry rushes and grass.

The Books were presented, as it would seem, at the instigation of His Excellency IWAKURA TOMOMI, who had learned, when in this country, that such a gift would be highly appreciated, and had promised to bring the matter to the notice of His Government on his return home.

The entire series of Books is contained in 103 cases or covers *(Ch'hih)*; in each case there are, on an average, 20 volumes, so that the entire number of volumes is rather more than 2,000.

Each of these volumes is divided into chapters *(p'hin)*,* according to the size of the volume. In some cases there are upwards of 15 short SÛTRAS in one volume. On the other hand there are some lengthy SÛTRAS, which occupy more than 20 volumes.

Placed one above the other, the Books in the collection would reach to a height of about 110 feet. In other words, they would require eleven shelves, of 10 feet in length each, if placed in a Library. When bound, however, they would occupy considerably less space.

There are several ways in which a Catalogue of these works might be arranged, or a Report framed of their contents.

1. They might be classified under the accepted division of VINAYA, SÛTRA, and ABHIDHARMA; but in this case a large number of miscellaneous works would have to be commented on or excepted; such would be all those of Chinese origin† and others, comprising Commentaries, Indexes and Treatises of a mixed character, which frequently occur in the midst of the collection. So that this arrangement would not be entirely satisfactory, or adapted for easy reference.

---

* The volumes themselves are called by the term *Kiouen*, but within the volume there may be several other distinct works, each of which is again divided into *Kiouen* (Chapters), and sometimes into Sections *(p'hin.)*

† The travels of the Buddhist Pilgrims, for example, are arranged under the heading of *King* or *Sûtras*, but it is evident that this arrangement is purely Chinese, and comparatively modern.

2. The method employed in the original division of the books, viz., by "determining characters" taken from the Thousand-letter Classic might be adopted, were it not that this arrangement is entirely artificial, and not familiar to the Western Student.

3. A more easy and ready method would be simply to take the works in the order of the Index, which forms the first CASE or COVER of the 103. But this would require an entire re-adjustment of the contents of the covers, and might lead to confusion.

4. The method, therefore, adopted is a simple and natural one. The several CASES or COVERS will be dealt with consecutively, from No. 1 to No. 103, and the contents noted, so far as is possible, with the titles of the several works appended. The cases themselves will then be *backed* with numbers corresponding to those in the Catalogue. In this way reference will be rendered easy, and the order of the Books, as received from Japan, not disturbed.

CASE I.

Two Volumes, with the distinguishing characters, *keen* and *kwan*, heaven and earth, *i.e.*, first and second. The two volumes divided into four Chapters (two in each volume.)

TITLE.

Ta-Ming-san-ts'ang-shing-kiau-muh-lu.

Index of the Holy Teaching of the TRIPITAKA, according to the arrangement made during the great MING dynasty.

CONTENTS OF VOLUME I.

(1) On the fly-leaf, as throughout the entire series of books, a figure of Buddha seated on a Lotus placed on a Throne, his right hand elevated, the thumb, first and fourth fingers raised, the two middle fingers bent inwards, the left hand bent downwards upon the stomach. On his breast the sign of the *Swastika*. On the forehead the *Urna*. His head with a singular ring of hair and the centre bald (or elevated), resembling the usual priestly tonsure. On the right and left the figures of KASYAPA and RAHULA, fully robed and closely shaven. Around the figure of Buddha a sea of flame or glory.

On the opposite side of the leaf is the usual dragon tablet *(lung p'ai)*, with the inscription "(May) the Imperial authority (plan) be ever firm, the judicial (kingly) authority illustrious, the Sun of Buddha wax brighter and brighter, and the wheel of the Law (Religion) ever revolve."

(2) The Japanese Preface, dated the 6th year of IM-PO, after this the Preface of TEN-WA *(Vide supra)*.

(3) Index of contents (*i.e.*, the contents of the entire collection).

1st. Three Imperial (Chinese) prefaces, viz.:—1. That by the Emperor WAN-LIEH of the MING dynasty. 2. That by CHUNG-TSUNG of the TANG dynasty (684 A.D.) 3. That by TAE-TSUNG of the SUNG dynasty (976 A.D.)

2nd. Books included under the letters of the Thousand-letter Classic, from *Tien* to *Nien*; these are—

I. Sûtras *(a)* of the Great Vehicle, classed as follows :—

CHAPTER I.

(1) Prajna Paramita collection; 72 *han* or *envelopes*. [The symbol *han* does not necessarily correspond to *ch'hih*, although having a similar meaning.]

(2) Ratnakûta collection; 17 *han*.

(3) Ta-tsa collection (*i.e.*, "Great miscellaneous collection," translated by Stas. Julien, "*Vaipulyasûtra. ou, sûtras dévellopés.*" *Concordance Sinico-samskrite*, p. 377; but the collection probably corresponds with that known in the South as "Nipâta" or "Sannipâta" Sûtras); 14 *han*.

(4) Avatamsaka collection; 22 *han*.

(5) Nirvana collection; 10 *han*.

(6) Other duplicate translations of various works contained in the preceding five collections; 42 *han*.

(7) Single translations; 79 *han*.

Total in the first Volume of the Index, 206 *han*, comprising 2061 chapters or *kiouen*.

CHAPTER II.

Books denoted with the thousand-classic letters from *t'so* to *chhuen* :—

I. Sûtras *(a)* of the Little Vehicle (Hinayâna).

(1) The Agama collection; 28 *han*.

(2) Single translations; 17 *han*.

(3) Other Sûtras, both of the Great and Little Vehicle, first admitted into the Canon during the Sung and Yuen dynasties; 22 *han*.

Total in the 2nd chapter of the Index, 67 *han*, comprising 670 chapters or *kiouen*.

CHAPTER III. VOLUME II.

Books denoted by characters from *lau* to *pw'an* :—

I. Sûtras admitted into the Canon during the Sung and Yuen dynasties beyond those already alluded to; 12 *han*.

II. Vinaya *(a)* of the Great Vehicle; 5 *han* : *(b)* of the Little Vehicle; 48 *han*.

III. Abhidharma *(a)* of the Great Vehicle; 50 *han* : *(b)* of the Little Vehicle; 73 *han*.

Total number of works named in the Volume III. 188 *han*, comprising 1860 chapters.

CHAPTER IV. VOLUME II.

Includes works noted by characters, from *chun* to *tsih.*

(a) Works of the ABHIDHARMA class admitted into the Canon during the SUNG ar YOUEN dynasties; 5 *han.*

(b) Works of a narrative character, relating to the Western Region (Sukhavati 19 *han.*

(c) Other works of the same character; 191 *han.*

Total, 175 *han*; 1750 Chapters.

Beyond the above, others, denoted by the characters included from *kin* to *shi*, ar introduced into the Canon during the MING dynasty; 41 *han* (410 Chapters.)

Grand Total of all Books, either now existing, or those lost, included in the Can(677 *han*; 6771 *kiouen.*

II.

Mo-ho-pan-jo-po-lo-mi-king.

The Mahâprajnaparamitâ Sûtra.

Translated by Hiouen Thsang. 20 volumes; from *Kiouen* 1 to 100. (*Vid.* Vie (Hiouen Thsang, pp. 338, 339, ss.)

III.

Ta-pan-jo-po-lo-mi-to-king.

The Mahâprajnapâramitâ Sûtra.

Translated by Hiouen Thsang. 20 volumes; from Kiouen 100 to Kiouen 200.

IV.

Ta-pan-jo-po-lo-mi-king.

The Mahâprajnapâramitâ Sûtra.

Translated by Hiouen Thsang. [Continuation of forenamed down to Kiouen 300.]

V.

Ta-pan-jo-po-lo-mi-king.

20 volumes. Continuation of above down to Kiouen 400.

VI.

Ta-pan-jo-po-lo-mi-king.

Contains 20 volumes of the Mahâprajnapâramita Sûtra. Translated by Hiouen Thsang (to Kiouen 500.)

VII.

Ta-pan-jo-po-lo-mi king.

Continuation and conclusion of the above (to Kiouen 600.)

VIII.

Mo-ho-pan-jo-po-lo-mi-to-king.

Mahâprajnaparamita.

Translated by Kumârajiva and another (*circ.* A.D. 400.) 9 Volumes; 30 Kiouen.

Fang-kwong-pan-jo-po-lo-mi-king.

The light emitting Prajna Paramita Sûtra

Translated by Dharmaraksha and Chu-shuh-lan, of the Western Tsin dynasty (230 A.D.) 6 Volumes; 30 Kiouen.

Kwong-tsan-pan-jo-po-lo-mi-king.

Stas. Julien (*Concordance* 218), quotes this as the same as the Prajna Paramita Sûtra

Translated by Chu-Fa-hu (The Indian DHARMAGUPTA (?)), of the Western Tsin dynasty (*circ.* 270 A D.) 3 Volumes; 10 Kiouen.

Taou-hing-pan-jo-po-lo-mi-king.

Another copy of the same work, in 3 Volumes; 10 Kiouen. Translated during the after Han dynasty.

Mo-ho-pan-jo-po-lo-mi-chao-king.

Dasasahasrikâ Prajnapâramitâ.

(*Jul., Concord.* 365.) 2 Volumes; 5 Kiouen. Translated by Chu-Fo-nien and others of the Tsin dynasty.

Ta-ming-to-wou-kie-king.

The Sûtra called "Ming-to-wou-kie," the name of a Bôdhisatwa. 1 Volume; 6 Kiouen

[*The remaining works in this case belong to the Prajna Paramita class*]

IX.

Ta-pao-tsih-king.

Mahâratnakûta Sûtra.

A voluminous compilation translated by Bôdhirutchi, of the Tang dynasty. 25 Volumes to Kiouen 100.

X.

To-pao-tsih-king.

Ratnakûta Sûtra.

Four Volumes, viz., from Kiouen 101 to Kiouen 120. Translated by Bôdhirutchi o the Tang dynasty.

Won-liang-tsing-sing-ping-tang-hioh-king.

The Sûtra which relates to the infinite and perfectly pure and equally diffused wisdon of Buddha.

Translated by Chi-lau-kia-ch'ai, belonging to the Getœ, during the after Han dynasty 1 Volume; 3 parts, pp. 28, 21, 24.

Tai-fang-kwang-san-kiai-king.

The Sûtra of the three Moral Rules, according to the expanded (vaipulya) school o division.

Translated by Dharmaraksha, of the Northern Liang dynasty. 1 Volume; 3 Parts

Ju-hwan-san-mei-king.

The Samâdhi, or meditation, called *ju-hwan, i.e*, like an illusion.

Translated by Dharmagupta, of the Western Tsin dynasty. 1 Volume; 3 Parts.

(a) Fuh-shwo-O-mi-to-king.

The Amitâbha Sûtra.

Translated by the Upasikawa Chi-hien, of the Wu period 2 Kiouen.

(b) Fuh-shwo-wou-liang-sheu-king.

The Sûtra of measureless years. 1 Volume; 2 Parts.

(a) Fo-shwo-O-yu-Fo-kwo-king.

The Sûtra of the land of Akshobya.

Translated by Chi-lau-kia-ch'ai, of the after Han dynasty. 1 Volume; 3 Parts

(b) **Fo-shwo-tai-shing-shi-fa-king.**

The Mahâyana dasadharmaka Sûtra. 1 Kiouen.

(a) **Man-ju-sse-li-Fo-t'u-yen-tsing-king.**

Manjusri (speaks) the Sûtra called the pure and glorious earth of Buddha.

Translated by Dharmagupta, of the Western Tsin dynasty. 2 Parts.

(b) **Fo-shwo-pau-t'oi-king.**

A Sûtra on the character of conception and parturition. By (as before.)

(c) **Fa-keng-king.**

Translated by two Religious persons of the after Han dynasty. 1 Kiouen; 2 Parts.

[*Six other Volumes, containing 23 short Sûtras, of no importance.*]

XI.

Ta-fang-teng-ta-tsi-king.

Mahâvaipulya mahâ sannipâta Sûtra. (?)

[Literally, a miscellaneous collection (of Sûtras), belonging to the expanded system c Buddhist Teaching.]

Translated by Dharmaraksha, of the Northern Liang dynasty. 9 Volumes; 30 Kiouen

Ta-tsi-ti-ts'ang-shi-lun-king.

Mahâvaipulya bhumigarbha dasachakra Sûtra. (?)

Translated by Hiouen Thsang. 3 Volumes; 10 Kiouen.

Ta-fang-teng-yue-ts'ang-king.

Chandragarbha mahâyana Sûtra.

Translated by Nalandayasa. 3 Volumes; 10 Kiouen.

Ta-fang-teng-ts'ang-king.

Suryagarbha mahâyana Sûtra.

Translated by Nalandayasa. 3 Volumes; 10 Kiouen.

Ta-fang-kwang-shi-lun-king.

Dasachakra Kchitigarbha. (*Julien.*)

Translator's name lost. 2 Volumes; 8 Kiouen.

Ta-tsi-su-mi-ts'ang-king.

Sumerugarbha vaipulya Sûtra. (?)

Translated by Nalandayasa and another. 1 Volume; 3 Parts.

XII.

A-cha-mo-pu-sah-king.

Aryakcharamati nirdesa nama mahayana Sûtra (Julien, *Concordance* 851.)

Translated by Dharmaraksha, of the Western Tsin dynasty. 1 Volume; 7 Kiouen.

Tai-tsa-pi-u-wang-king.

Mahasannipâta avadana râja Sûtra.

Translated by Djnanakûta, of the Tsui dynasty. 1 Volume; 2 Parts.

Ta-fang-teng-nien-Fo-san-mui-king.

Mahavaîpulya Buddhanusmritti samadhi Sûtra.

Translated by Dharmajita, of the Tsin dynasty. 2 Volumes; 10 Kiouen.

Pou-sah-nien-Fo-sam-mui-king.

Same as above. 2 Volumes; 6 Kiouen.

Pa'o-sing-to-lo-ni-king.

The Dharani of Pao-sing (precious star.)

Translated by Prabhamitra, of the Tang dynasty. 2 Volumes; 8 Kiouen.

Pa'o-niu-so-wan-king.

Questions of Pa'o-niu (precious woman.)

Translated by Dharmaraksha of the Western Tsin dynasty. 1 Volume; 4 Kiouen.

Wou-yen-chong-tseu-king.

Sutra of the dumb boy.

1 Volume; 2 Parts. Translated (as above.)

Ta'-gae-king.

Great pity Sûtra (Mahâkarunika).

Translated as before. 2 Volumes; 8 Kiouen.

Ta-fang-teng-ta-tsa-hien-hu-king.

Mahâvaîpulya mahâ sannipâta bhadrapâla Sûtra. 1 Volume ; 5 Kiouen.

Translated by Djnanakûta and another, of the Tsui dynasty.

Pan-chow-san-mui-king.

The same work as the former (according to Stas. Julien, *Concordance* 404).

Translated during the after Han dynasty. 1 Volume ; 3 Parts.

(*a*) **Hiu-k'ong-ing-pu-sah-king.**

Aryâkâsagarbha nâma mahâyâna Sûtra. (*Julien, Concordance* 196.)

Translated by Djnanakûta of the Tsui dynasty.

(*b*) **Hiu-k'ong-ts'ang-pu-sah-king.**

Akâsagarbha bôdhisatwa Sûtra.

Translated as before.

(*c*) **Hiu-k'ong-ts'ang-pu-sah-shin-chau-king.**

Akâsagarbha bôdhisatwa dhârani Sûtra.

Translated by Dharmamitra of the Sung dynasty.

(*d*) **Kwan-hiu-k'ong-ts'ang-pu-sah-king.**

Same as (*b*).

The above *a*, *b*, *c*, *d*, in one Volume.

[*Three Volumes*, 1, 2, 3, *containing other Sutras of small importance*].

XIII.

Ta-fang-kwang-Fo-fa-yan-king.

Buddhâvatamsaka vaîpulya Sûtra.

In 60 Kiouen ; 20 Volumes. Translated by Buddhabhadra and others, of the Eastern Tsin dynasty. 317-419 A.D.

XIV.

Ta-fang-kwang-Fo-fa-yan-king.

The Buddhâvatamsaka Sutra.

Translated by Sikshananda, of Khoten, who flourished during the Tang dynasty. 24 Volumes; 80 Kiouen.

XV.

Ta-shi-twan-kie-king.

A work in 4 Volumes and 14 kiouen, of the Great Vehicle, translated by Fo-nien (Buddhasmitti.) [I do not know the Sanscrit Title.]

Fo-shwo-Fo-ming-king.

Buddha recites the names of all the Buddhas. 3 Volumes; 12 Kiouen.

Translated by Bodhirutchi, of the Wei period.

Fo-shwo-sheu-leng-yan-san-mui-king.

The Surângama samâdhi Sutra. 1 Volume; 3 Parts.

Translated by Kumarajiva.

Wu-tsien-wu-pih-Fo-ming-king.

The names of 5,500 Buddhas. 2 Volumes; 8 Kiouen.

Translated by two Priests of the Tsui dynasty, Kuta and Gupta.

To-shai-p'hin-king.

A chapter from the Avatamsaka Sutra, so called. 2 Volumes; 6 Kiouen.

Hien-kie-king.

Bhadrakalpika Sûtra.

Translated by Dharmarakshita. 3 Volumes; 10 Kiouen.

Tching-yang-tchou-Fo-kong-te-king.

Kusuma sanichaya Sutra (*Concordance* 703) 1 Volume; 3 Parts.

Translated by two Indian Priests during the Wei period.

(a) **Mi-tsang-yeou-in-un-king.**

The events or causes that led to exhibition of wonderful (miraculous) power by Buddha

Translated by Dharmaraksha, of the Western Tsin dynasty.

(b) **Tchu-Fo-iu-tsi-king.**

Various extracts from the different Buddhas. (Buddha sangiti *n.m.y.* Sutra *Concordance* 720).

Translated as above. 2 Parts.

(a) **Mo-ho-mo-ye-king.**

Mahamaya Sutra.

This is otherwise called " Buddha's ascent into Heaven to preach to his mother."

(b) **Tchu-te-fuh-tin-king.**

Ratnajali paripritche'ha.

Translated by two Priests of the Western Tsin dynasty.

(c) **Ta-fang-teng-ju-lai-king.**

Tathâgata garbha *n.m.y.* Sutra. (*Concordance* 606).

Translated by Buddhabhadra, of the Eastern Tsin dynasty.

(d) **Fo-shwo-pao-wang-king.**

Ratnajala Sutra.

Translated by Dharmaraksha, of the Western Tsin dynasty.

(a) **Kwan-shai-yin-pou-sah-teh-ta-shai-sheu-ki-king.**

The record of the oath of Kwan-yin to save the world.

(b) **Pou-sse-i-kwong-pu-sah-sho-shwo-king.**

Aryâchintyaprabhâsa nirdesa *n.m.y.* Sutra. *Vide Concordance* 495.

(c) **Chiu-jih-ming-san-mui-king.**

The Sâmadhi called the " Brightness of the Dawn " (*vikramâditya*,) (*d*) **Tchou-kong-tsai-wan-king.**

Srikantha Sûtra (?) (*Julien, Concordance* 724.)

(*a*) **Pou-sah-taou-shu-king.**

Bôdhisatwa bôdhidruma Sutra

(*b*) **Pou-sah-sing-ti-king.**

Kchâmâkara Bôdhisatwa Sutra (*Julien, Concordance* 484.)

(*c*) **Wou-heou-tseng-kwong-king.**

Vimaladhàrani Sutra. (?)

[*And three other short Sutras in the same Volume of no importance.*]

Kiu-king.

Nine Sutras; among which are two Translations of the Ratnajâli paripritchch'a. (*Concordance* 479.)

XVI.

Ta-pan-ni-pwan-king.

The Mahâparinirvâna Sutra.

Translated by Dharmalatsin (or, 'raksha'), of the Northern Liang dynasty. 15 Volumes; 40 Caps.

XVII.

Nan-pen-ta-pan-ni-pwan-king.

The Mahâparinirvana Sutra according to the Southern original [*i.e.*, the Southern translation, or the translation made for the Southern copy of the Tripitaka.]

Eight Volumes, from Kiouen 11 to Kiouen 36. Translated from Sanscrit (Fan) by the Priest Dharmaraksha, of the Northern Liang dynasty.

Ta-pan-ni-pwan-king.

The Mahaparinirvana Sutra.

Translated by Fahien, in connection with the Hindoo Buddhabhadra, during the Eastern Tsin dynasty. 2 Volumes; 6 Kiouen.

Ta-pan-ni-pan-king-heou-fen.

The after-division of the Mahâparinirvâna Sûtra.

This contains the last events before the death of Buddha, and the contention for his relics.

Translated by Jnanabhadra and others, of the Tang dynasty. 1 Volume; 2 Parts; pp. 20 and 22.

Fang-teng-pan-ni-pwan-king.

The Parinirvana Sûtra *expanded* (vaîpulya).

By Dharmagupta, of the Western Tsin dynasty. 1 Volume; 2 Parts; pp. 34 and 26.

Ta-pei-king.

Mahâkarunika Sûtra.

Translated by Nalandaryasa, of the period Kao-Tsai. 1 Volume; 5 Kiouen.

(a) **Ta-pan-ni-pwan-king.**

Mahâparinirvâna Sûtra.

Translated by Fahien, of the Eastern Tsin dynasty. 3 Parts; pp. 19, 21, 20.

(b) **Fang-tang-ni-pwan-king.**

Another copy of the above. Translator's name lost. 2 Parts; pp. 27 and 28.

Wu-king.

Five Sûtras.

(a) **Sz-chung-tseu-san-mui-king.**

The Samâdhi of the four youths.

Translated by Djnanakûta, of the Tsui dynasty. 2 Parts; pp. 20, 19, 20.

(b) **Fuh-shing-pan-ni-pwan-shwo-kiau-kiai-king.**

Last words of Buddha before entering Nirvana.

Translated by Kumarajiva. pp. 7.

(c) Fuh-lam-ni-pan-ki-fa-chu-king.

Records concerning the endurance of the Law, delivered before the Nirvana.

Translated by Hiouen Thsang, of the Tang dynasty. [*He speaks of the* 1,000 *yea after the Nirvana, as the scene of progress and triumph; after this the cause of Religi begins to fail.*] pp. 5.

(d) Fuh-mie-to-hau-kwan-hom-tsang-sung-king.

Rules for the correct burial of the body (relics) of Buddha.

This is an interesting Sûtra, containing the Rules for the burial of a Chakrvartt Monarch (*fei-hing-wong-ti, i.e.*, a King who "flies as he goes"); and also an account the Patra of Buddha, and the mode of recovering it, bearing a strong resemblance to t legend of the Sangreal.

Translator's name lost: found in the Western Tsin Catalogue. pp. 3.

(e) Pan-ni-pwan-heou-kun-lah-king.

Worship or sacrifices to be offered after the Nirvana.

Translated by Dharmagupta, of the Western Tsin dynasty. p. 1.

XVIII.

(a) Fa-hwa-san-mui-king.

A Sûtra respecting Samâdhi, called "(Sad) dharma pundarika."

Translated by Che-yen, of the Sung dynasty. 1 Part; pp. 15.

(b) Saddharma pundarika Sutra.

[A section of the larger Sûtra. It appears to be an early translation, as it is four among the Books in the Western Tsin Catalogue. Observe, Feou-to is, in this translatio used for "*Pagoda*," and not for "*Buddha*."] 1 Part; pp. 4.

(c) Kwan-shai-yin-ph'o-men-p'in-king.

The *Samanta mukha* section of the Saddharma pundarika Sûtra.

Translated by Kumarajiva. pp. 7.

Ching-fa-hwa-king.

The Saddharma Pundarika Sûtra

Translated by Chu-fa-hu, *i.e.*, Dharmagupta, of the Western Tsin dynast 3 Volumes; 10 Caps.

Min-fa-lien-king.

Another version of the above, by Kumarajiva, of the period Yaou-tsin. 2 Volume 7 Kiouen.

Kin-kwong-ming-king.

The Survana prabhâsa Sutra.

Translated by Dharmalatsin, of the North Liang dynasty. 1 Volume; 4 Kiouen.

Ho-po-kin-kwong-ming-king.

Another version of the above, by Djnanakûta, of the Tsui dynasty. (Observe th Djnanakûta is translated by *Chi-tih*, and not by *Tih-chi*, as generally is done 2 Volumes; 8 Kiouen.

Kin-kwong-ming-tsui-shing-wang-king.

Another version, by I-tsing, of the Tang dynasty. 2 Volumes; 10 Kiouen.

(a) Teng-tsi-chung-tih-san-mui-king.

A Sutra on Samâdhi. 2 Parts; pp. 20 and 19.

(b) Tsi-yih-tsai-fuh-tih-san-mui-king.

Another Sutra on Samâdhi. 1 Part; pp. 19.

Wou-liang-i-king.

A Sutra called 'measureless Truth' (paramartha.) (?)

By Dharmagatayasa, of the Kan Tsai period. 1 Volume; pp. 16.

(a) Jih-teng-puh-teng-yin-king.

A Sutra on Samâdhi, and that which is not Samadhi.

Translated by I-tsing, of the Tang dynasty. pp. 20.

(b) Pu-pih-teng-jih-teng-jih-yin-king.

On Samâdhi.

By Dharmaprajnaruchi, of the Wei dynasty. pp. 25.

XIX.

A-wei-yue-chi-cha-king.

Aryâparivarttya *n m.* Sutra. (*Concordance* 40.)

Translated by Dharmagupta, of the Western Tsin dynasty. 1 Volume; 4 Kiouen.

Luh-lo-t'sa-king.

A Sûtra containing various extracts of Bôdhisatwa's conduct whilst fulfilling th 6 Paramitas. 3 Volumes; 8 Kiouen.

Fo-shwo-po-yun-king.

Ratnamegha *n.m.* Sûtra. (*Concordance* 421.) 3 Volumes; 10 Kiouen.

Translated by Dharmarutchi, of the Tang dynasty.

Pei-hwa-king.

Karunapundarika Sûtra. (*Concordance* 431.) 3 Volumes; 10 Kiouen.

Translated by Dharmaraksha, of the Northern Liang dynasty.

(*a*) Fo-shwo-po-yun-king.

The 6th or 7th Kiouen of the Ratnamegha Sutra.

Fo-shing-to-li-tien-wei-moo-shwo-fa-king.

Buddha ascends to the 33 Heavens to preach for his Mother's Salvation.

Translated by Dharmagupta, of the Western Tsin dynasty. [The 2 above in 1 Volume.

(*a*) Ta-shing ting-wang-king.

Vimalakirtta Nirdesa. (*Concordance* 594.)

(*b*) Ta-fang-kwang-ting-wang-king.

Vimalakirtti Nirdesa *n.m.y.s.* (*Concordance* 616.)

[But it ought to be *vaipulyam.*] (The above in 1 Volume.)

Theen-pwan-miu-fa-lin-hwa-king.

A section of the Saddharma pundarika Sutra [called "Theen," *i.e.*, increase.] or i appears to be a translation of the whole Book. Compare the last chapter, 27 with the "*Lotus.*"

Translated by Djnanakuta and Dharmagupta, of the Tsui dynasty.

Wei-ma-kih-sho-shwo-king.

Vimalakirtti Sûtra. 1 Volume.

[Also called Puh-ho-sze-i-kiai-tuh-king.] Translated by Kumarajiva.

Wei-mo-kih-king.

The same as above.

Translated during the Wu period.

Shwo-wou-hu-ching-king.

Same as above.

Translated by Hiouen Thsang, of the Tang dynasty.

(a) **Fen-pih-un-hi-cho-shing-fa-men-king.**

(b) **Un-sing-cho-shing-fen-fa-pen-king.**

[The two in one Volume.]

Tao-shan-shuh-wou-k'i-lo-fa-king.

Various apparitional changes of Bôdhisatwa. 1 Volume; 4 Kiouen.

XX.

Fang-kwang-ta-chwang-yan-king.

This is a Chinese Version of the *Lalita Vistara* Sûtra.

In four Books; 12 Chapters *(Kiouen)*; 27 Sections *(Vaggas, or p'hin)*.

Translated by the Shaman Devakara, of the Tang dynasty.

The following is a brief analysis of the contents of this Book, compared with the corresponding account found in the French Translation from the Thibetan, by M. Foucaux

Section 1; Kiouen 1—Introduction (*French*—Sujet du discours).

Section 2; Kiouen 1—Heavenly Palace in the Tusita Heaven (*French*—Changement de séjour).

Section 3; Kiouen 1—Excellent Family, or Caste (*French*—Pureté complète de race)

Section 4 ; Kiouen 1—Modes of Salvation (*French*—Portes évidentes de la loi).

Section 5 ; Kiouen 2—Coming down to be born (*French*—Descente (du ciel) Touchita).

Section 6 ; Kiouen 2—Incarnation (*French*—Entrée dans le sein d'une mère).

Section 7 ; Kiouen 3—Birth (*French*—Naissance).

Section 8 ; Kiouen 4—Entering the Deva Temple (*French*—Visite au Temple des Dieux).

Section 9 ; Kiouen 4—Presentation of gifts (*French*—Ornements du Bôdhisattva).

Section 10 ; Kiouen 4—Instruction in Books or Writing (*French*—L' école d' écriture).

Section 11 ; Kiouen 4—Beholding the ploughing match (*French*—Village de l' agriculture).

Section 12 ; Kiouen 4—Exhibition of ability (*French*—Epreuve de l'habilité dans les arts).

Section 13 ; Kiouen 5—Strains of music excite reflection (*French*—Exhortation).

Section 14 ; Kiouen 5—Excited by dreams (*French*—Songes).

Section 15 ; Kiouen 6—Leaving Home (*French*—Entrée dans le monde).

Section 16 ; Kiouen 7—The exhortation of Bimbasara Râja (*French*—Visite de Vimbasara.)

Section 17 ; Kiouen 7—Sufferings from austerities (*French*—Pratique des austérités).

Section 18 ; Kiouen 7—Advance to the Nairanjana River (*French*—La rivière Nairanjana).

Section 19 ; Kiouen 8—Arrival at the enclosure (mandala) of the Bôdhi Tree (*French*—Marche vers Bôdhimanda).

Section 20 ; Kiouen 8—Decorating the enclosure of the Bôdhi Tree (*French*—Evolutions de Bôdhimanda).

Section 21 ; Kiouen 9—Overcoming Mâra (*French*—Défaite du Démon).

Section 22 ; Kiouen 9—Arriving at perfect Enlightenment (*French*—Revétissement de l' intelligence parfaite et accomplie).

Section 23 ; Kiouen 10—Exhortation in laudatory verses (*French*—Louanges).

Section 24 ; Kiouen 10—The Record of the Merchants (*French*—Trapoucha et Bhallika).

Section 25 ; Kiouen 10—Solicitation of Brahma Râja (*French*—Exhortation).

Section 26 *(a)*; Kiouen 11—Turning the wheel of the Law (*French*—Action de tourner la roue de la loi).

Section 26 *(b)*—Turning the wheel of the Law. [The French has no such division.]

Section 27 ; Kiouen 12—Entrusting to the charge of others (*French*—Conclusion).

It will be seen from this how closely the Chinese and the Thibetan and Sanscrit versions agree ; and from a comparison of the contents of the Chapters, this agreement is still more evident.

Pou-yaou-king.

Universal Light.

This is another version of the Lalita Vistara. 2 Volumes ; 8 Chapters ; 30 Sections.

Translated by the Indian Priest, Dharmaraksha, during the Western Tsin period (265-313 A.D.)

[The contents of this work are accurately given in M. Senart's *Legende du Bouddha*, p. 497, *n*. 4.]

Kwang-po-yen-tsing-pou-tui-chun-fa-lun-king.

Aryvâarttya nama mahayana Sûtra. 1 Volume ; 4 Chapters.

Translated by Ratnamegha and another, of Liang-chow, during the Sung dynasty.

Chu-fa-pen-wou-king.

Sarvadharma pravritti nirdesa Sûtra.

Translated by Djnanakuta, of the Tsui dynasty. 1 Volume ; 3 Parts.

Ta-shu-kin-na-lo-wang-sho-man-king.

Mahadruma kinnararaja paripritchch'a.

Translated by Kumârajiva. 1 Volume ; 4 Kiouen.

Pou-tui-chun-fa-lun-king.

Arya aparivarttya Sutra. *(Julien, Concordance 501.)* 1 Volume ; 4 Chapters.

[No Translator's name given.]

Tun-chin-to-lo-sho-wen-king.

1 Volume; 3 Parts. Translated by Chi-lu-kia, of the after Han dynasty.

Tchi-shai-king.

Dharmamudra Sûtra. 1 Volume; 4 Parts.

Translated by Kumârajiva.

(a) Tchu-fa-wou-hing-king.

Sarvadharma pravritti nirdesa Sûtra. (?)

Translated by Kumârajiva

(b) Tchi-jin-pu-sah-sho-wen-king.

Same as Dharmamudra Sûtra.

Translated by Dharmaraksha of the Western Tsin dynasty. (The above, *a* and *b*, in or Volume.)

(a) Siang-sou-kia-to-ti-po-lo-liu-i-king.

(b) Siang-sou-kia-to-tsui-shun-chu-liu-i-king.

(c) Fo-shwo-kiai-tsih-king.

The three foregoing, in one Volume, are translations of various Chapters of the Sandl nirmochana (or, nimorchani) Sûtra. Vide *Julien*, *Concordance* 275.

The first two (*a* and *b*), translated by Gunabhadra, of the Sung dynasty. The third (*c* by *Tchin-ti*, of the Tsui dynasty.

XXI.

Jih-leng-kia-king.

Lankâvatara Sûtra.

[Literally, *entering* Lanka Sûtra. Observe the similarity in the name of Vishnu, fro *Vis*, "to enter."]

Translated by Bôdhirutchi, of the Wei dynasty. 3 Volumes; 10 Kiouen.

Ta-shing-jih-leng-kia-king.

Same as the above, with the addition of Mahâyana.

Translated by Sikshananda, of the Tang dynasty. 2 Volumes; 7 Kiouen.

Leng-kia-o-po-ta-lo-pao-king.

Lankâvatara mahâyana Sûtra.

Translated by Gunabhadra, of the Sung dynasty. 2 Volumes; 4 Kiouen.

Ta-sa-she-ni-kin-tseu-shen-ki.

The prophecy received by Mahaskini Kinnaraputra. 2 Volumes; 10 Kiouen.

Pu-sa-hing-fang-pin-pien-fa-king.

Different appearances assumed by Bôdhisatwa during his preparation for supreme Buddhaship.

Translated by Gunabhadra, of the Sung dynasty. 1 Volume; 3 Parts.

Fo-shwo-ta-kun-teng-shin-chau-king.

Dhârani to be said at the time of the Abhisheka Ceremony.

Translated during the Eastern Tsin dynasty. 2 Volumes; 12 Kiouen.

Fo-shwo-man-chu-si-li-in-p'ao-tsang.

Ta-fang-kwang-pao-sun-king.

Two Sûtras relating to Manjusri. 1 Volume; 2 Parts.

One other Volume, containing four short Sutras: the last called "The Ajatasatru Sutra;" the others relating to a fabulous Tathagata called "The Medicine Lord." 1 Volume.

XXII.

Yue-tang-san-mui-king.

The Samadhi called Tchandra-dipa (?) (Moon-lamp.)

In 3 Volumes; 11 Kiouen. Translated by Nalandayasa.

Tai-pei-fen-to-li-king.

Mahâ karuna pundarika Sûtra.

2 Volumes; 8 Kiouen. Translator's name lost.

Tchi-sin-fan-tien-sho-man-king.

Arya visechachinti Brahma paripritchch'a (*Julien, Concordance* 691).

Translated by Chu-fa-hu (Dharmaraksha), of the Western Tsin dynasty. 1 Volume 4 Kiouen.

Ching-sse-wei-Fan-tien-sho-man-king.

Arya visechachinti Brahmana paripritchch'a Sutra tika. (*Julien, Concordance* 110.)

1 Volume; 6 Kiouen. Translated by Bodhirutchi.

Sse-yih-Fan-tien-sho-man-king.

Arya visechachinti Brahma paripritchch'a; or, otherwise, Brahmavisechachinti pari pritchch'a. (*Julien, Concordance* 551.)

Translated by Kumarajiva. 1 Volume; 4 Kiouen.

Shen-sse-t'ong-tseu-king.

Vimalakirtti nirdesa. [*Julien. Concordance* 60.] 1 Volume complete.

Translated by Djnanakuta.

(*a*) P'o-chau-san-mui-king.

The samadhi called "All excelling."

(*b*) Fang-poh-king.

Ajatasatru kaukrittya vinichudana. (*Concordance* 149).

The two before-named in one volume. The first translated by Dharmaraksha, of the Western Tsin dynasty. The second, which is the same (according to the Tika) as the second section of the previous Sutra, translated by an unknown editor.

(*a*) Fo-shwo-ta-tseng-fa-men-king.

(*b*) Ta-chwang-yen-fa-men-king.

These are evidently two translations of the same work. They are referred to by (*Julien Concordance* 658), but no Sanscrit Title is given, unless, in 654, *Ming* is a mistake for *Men*, in which case the Title is "Manjusri vikridita Sutra."

Ta-fang-teng-ta-yun-tsing-u-king.

Mahamega *n.m.y.* Sutra, according to (*Julien, Concordance* 61

But in other works it is restored Arya-maha-megha-mandalavarsha-vardd na-Sutra.

There are two other versions of the same Sutra bound up in one . ei

The first translated by Djnanakuta and others. The second by Djnanayas The third by Nalandayasa. [The third is that which I have translated in the "Catena f Buddhist Scriptures," p. 416, and ss.]

(a) Yue-tang-san-mui-king.

This is the same as the 8th Kiouen of the preceding "Moon-lamp" Samâ i.

Translated by a Shaman called Sien-kung.

(b) Fo-shwo-siang-ye-king.

Hastikakchya Sutra (*Julien, Concordance* 523).

Translated by Dharmamita.

(c) Fo-shwo-wou-sho-hi-tsam-king.

Same as Siang-pou-king, *i.e.*, Hastikakchyâ Sutra (Vid. sup.)

Translated by Dharmaraksha, of the Western Tsin dynasty.

[The three above-named in one Volume.]

(a) Fo-shwo-ta-shing-t'ong-sing-king.

Mahayana abhisamaya Sutra. (*Julien, Concordance* 595.)

(b) Ching-kie-ta-shing-king.

Otherwise written Fo-shwo-ching &c.

Same as the previous Sutra, viz., the Mahayana abbisamaya Sutra. (*Vide Juli , Concordance* 695).

Translated by Devakara and others, during the Sung dynasty, with a Royal preface.

Luh-king.

Six Sutras, as follows:—

1. Kwan-wou-liang-sheu-Fo-king.

Amitabha vyuha *m.y.* Sutra (for other variations of Title, *Vide Julien, Concordance* 228).

Translated during the Sung dynasty.

2. Tching-tsan-seng-t'o-fo-shih-shau-king.

Sukhavati vyûha *m.y.* Sûtra.

Translated by Hiouen Thsang, of the Tang dynasty.

3. A-mi-to-king.

Amitâbha Sûtra.

4. Ta-a-mi-to-king.

Mahamitabha Sutra.

[And two others of the same kind.]

Kiu-king.

Nine short Sutras relating to the advent of Maitreya.

Pah-king.

Eight short Sûtras, among which the History of "Sâmaputra" and of the "Dumb Child" occur. In one Volume.

Shi-lu-king.

Sixteen short Sutras.

Among these is the "Anakchara granthaka rochana gârbha Sûtra," noted by *Stas. Julien, Concordance* 584 and 575 (different translations of the same work); the "Chandra-prâbha kumâra Sutra (do. 870); the Vatsaputra Sutra;" and the History of the Old Woman who spent her two mites to buy a candle to burn before the shrine of Buddha.

Shi-pah-king.

Eighteen Sutras.

They relate principally to the origin of Image Worship or Construction, and are well deserving attention. 1 Volume.

A Volume marked **F** on the cover, containing three Sutras of the Dhârani class. 1 Volume.

A Volume marked **H,** of the same kind.

A Volume marked **K,** of the same kind.

XXIII.

Ta-fang-teng-ta-yun-king.

Mahâ megha nâma mahâyana Sûtra.

Translated by Dharmalatsin, of the North Liang dynasty (beginning of 6th centur
1 Volume; 4 Kiouen.

Kiai-shan-mi-king.

Sandhi nirmochana nâma mahâyana Sûtra.

Translated by Hiouen Thsang, of the Tang dynasty. 1 Volume; 5 Kiouen.

Shan-kiai-t'u-king.

Same as above. (*Julien, Concordance* 96.)

Translated by Bodhirutchi, of the Wei period. 1 Volume; 5 Kiouen.

Jou-lai-chwang-yen-fuh-keng-kiai-king.

Tathagata garbha Sûtra. (?)

1 Volume; 2 Parts; pp. 19 and 21.

(*a*) **Fo-shwo-keen-wang-king.**

(*b*) **Jou-lai-shi-kiau-sheng-kwan-wang-king.**

(*c*) **Fo-wai-sheng-kwong-tien-tseu-shwo-wang-fa-king.**

(*d*) **Pa'o-tsih-san-mui-man-chu-sse-li-pu-sah-wan-fa-shin-king.**

(*e*) **Fo-shwo-tsai-chu-fang-teng-hioh-king.**

(*f*) **Ta-shing-fang-kwang-tsung-chi-king.**

(*g*) **Ta-tseu-su-ta-na-king.**

(*h*) **Fo-shwo-jou-lai-chi-in-king.**

The preceding eight Sutras are in one Volume.

The last (*h*) is the same as "Tathâgata jnana mudrâ."

The second relates to Prasenajit râja.

The seventh is the Mâhakumâra Sudana; or, a "History of the Royal Prince Sudana." It is the Wessantara Jâtaka fully told. 1 Volume; Eight Sûtras.

(a) Fo-shwo-hwui-in-san-mui-king.

The Djnana mu lra Samâdhi Sûtra.

(b) Fo-shwo-wou-kih-pa'o-san-mui-king.

(c) Pa'o-jou-lai-san-mui-king.

Three Sûtras on Samadhi. 1 Volume.

Shi-tsi-king.

Seventeen Sutras.

(a) Fo-shwo-kin-sih-niu-king.

Buddha declares the History of the Female called "Silver Color."

This is an extraordinary story of a girl who cut off her breasts to feed a starving woman who was going to devour her newly-born infant; in consequence of this, and the earnest vow she made, she was changed into a young man, and afterwards was adopted by Padmarâja and became a King, under the name 'Silver-color-king!'; afterwards he was born again in the world as a beautiful boy. He was Rahûla, &c.

(b) Fo-shwo-O-che-shai-wang-shau-kiuh-king.

Prediction given concerning Ajatasatru.

(c) Tsae-hwa-wei-wong-shang-Fo-shau-kiuh-king.

(d) Fo-shwo-ching-kung-kiau-king.

[A Sûtra relating sedate and respectful conduct.]

(e) Fo-shwo-shen-kung-kiau-king.

(f) Ch'hing-tsan-tai-shing-kung-tih-king.

Laudatory verses respecting the Great Vehicle (Mahâyana), by Hiouen Thsang.

(g) Miau-fa-kiuh-teng-nien-chang-king.

(h) Fo-shwo-pei-to-shu-hia-sz-wei-shi-i-yin-un-king.

Appears to be the Mahânidana Sûtra.

(i) Fo-shwo-un-hi-shing-tau-king.

A Sûtra on the causes leading to Supreme enlightenment. Translated by Hiouen Thsang.

(j) Fo-shwo-saou-kan-king.

(k) Fo-shwo-liu-muh-sing-sze-king.

(l) Fo-shwo-sze-shai-san-mui-king.

[With three others.]

The above brief Sutras are of some interest, and deserve examination.

The translations date from an early period, principally the Eastern Tsin dynasty, *circ.* 300 A.D.

Shi-i-king.

Twelve short Sûtras

Tsah-king.

Seven short Sûtras.

The third is the Gayasirsha Sûtra, composed by Vasubhandou, and translated by Bődhirutchi, during the Wei period, *circ.* 180 A.D.

[The other Sutras deserve examination.]

XXIV.

Fo-mou-ta-kong-tsio-ming-wang-king.

Mahâ mayuri vidya radjnî dharanî. 1 Volume; 3 Parts; pp. 28, 31, 17.

Fo-shwo-to-lo-ni-ts'a.

A collection of Dharani.

Translated by Atikuta, of the Tang dynasty. 4 Volumes; 13 Kiouen.

Suh-tung-Fo-muh-ta-kong-tsio-ming-wang-king.

Probably the same as that catalogued above: Mahâ mayuri vidyâ radjni dharanî. 1 Volume; 3 Parts.

Puh-hung-kiouen-so-chin-in-king.

Amoghapasa dharani.

Translated by Bôdhiruchi, of the Tang dynasty. 9 Volumes; 30 Kiouen.

Fo-shwo-kung-tsio-wang-chau-king.

Kung-tsio-wang-ts'a-shin-ts'a-king.

Kin-sih-kung-tsio-wang-chau-king.

Kung-tsio-wang-shin-chau-king.

Puh-hung-kiouen-so-chau-king.

Five Books, containing Dhâranis. They appear to be all connected with the Moriya, or Mora, Charms, and may probably be traced to the "Peacock Jataka." 1 Volume; 5 Kiouen.

[Another Volume, containing similar Dharanis, numbered **G** on the cover, follows.]

Shi-sz-king.

A Volume containing fourteen Sûtras, all belonging to the Dharani class. 1 Volume.

Shi-yih-king.

Eleven Sutras.

The first is called the Questionings of the Brahmachari "Shau-i" ('head thought.') The others contain Dharani, principally those known as Chunti (Chundi, or Durga.) 1 Volume.

Shi-king.

Ten Sutras; principally Dharanis. 1 Volume.

Pah-king.

Eight Sutras, containing Dharanis. 1 Volume.

H (so marked on cover), contains four Sutras of the Tantra class. 1 Volume.

XXV.

Ta-fang-kwang-ph'o-hien-hing-un-king.

A Section of the Avatamsaka Sutra.

Translated by Prajna (*sic*), of the Tang dynasty. 10 Volumes; 40 Kiouen.

Shi-chu-king.

Daçabhumi Sûtra. (?)

Translated by Kumârajiva and another. 2 Volumes; 6 Kiouen.

Sin-li-ji-in-fa-men-king.

Sraddhâbâla dhanâvatara mudra *n.m.y.* Sûtra. *(Concordance 527).*

1 Volume; 5 Kiouen. Translated by Dharmarutchi, of the Wei period.

Pou-sah-pen-teng-king.

Ugra paripritchch'a. (?)

Translated by a pious layman of the Western Tsin dynasty.

Pou-sah-shi-chu-hing-tao-p'en-king.

A section of the Avatamsaka Sûtra.

Fo-shwo-pu-sah-shi-chu-king.

A section from the Avatamsaka Sûtra.

(a) **Fo-fa-yan-puh-sse-i-keng-kiai-king.**

(b) **Fo-shwo-ju-lai-hing-hien-king.**

[The two above-named in one Volume.]

Lo-ma-kia-king.

Râmaka Sûtra. (?) 1 Volume; 4 Kiouen.

(a) **Teng-muh-pou-sah-sho-wen-san-mui-king.**

(b) **Wen-chu-sse-li-wen-pu-sah-shu-king.**

[The above-named in one Volume.]

Tsien-pi-yih-tsai-chi-te-king.

2 Volumes; 5 Kiouen. Translated by Dharmaraksha, of the Western Tsin dynasty.

Kwo-heu-choang-yan-kie-tsien-Fo-nung-king,

[And two others.] Names of Buddhas in the past, present, and future kalpas.

Shi-yih-king.

Eleven short Sûtras: among which is "The Heart of Bôdhi, a Sûtra;" "Bimbasara râja Sutra;" "Bôdhisatwa dasabhumi," &c.

XXVI.

Hwa-shau-king.

Kusala mûla samparigraha Sûtra.

Translated by Kumârajiva. 3 Volumes; 10 Kiouen.

Ta-wai-tih-to-lo-ni-king.

A Book containing Dhârani; or, charmed words.

Translated by Djnanakuta. 3 Volumes; 20 Kiouen.

Ta-fa-k'heu-to lo-ni-king.

A Book of Dhârani (the great Law-torch.)

Translated by Djnanakûta. 4 Volumes; 20 Kiouen.

Kwan-tsai-chu-fa-hing-king.

A work translated by Djnanakûta, on the comprehensive nature of Dharma. 1 Volume; 4 Kiouen.

Ta-fang-tang-to-lo-ni-king.

A Book on Samâdhi (Pratyoutpanna Buddha samamukhâvasthita Samâdhi. *Julien.*)

Translated by Fa-chung (Dharmasangha (?)). 1 Volume; 4 Kiouen.

Pah-king.

Eight short Sûtras [of no importance.] 1 Volume; pp. 42.

Li-choang-yan-san-mui-king.

A work on Samâdhi.

Translated by Nalandayasa, of the Tsui dynasty. 1 Volume.

XXVII.

Pu-sah-chu-t'oi-king.

Literally, "The Incarnation of Bôdhisatwa;" but it is a work of the Great Vehicle, and entirely speculative.

Translated by Buddhasmritti, of the Yao-tsin period (*circ.* 400 A.D.) 2 Volumes; 5 Kiouen.

Ta-Fo-ting-sheu-ling-yan-king.

The Surangama Sûtra.

Translated by Paramiti and Meghasikha. 2 Volumes; 10 Kiouen.

Fa-tsi-king.

Dharmasangiti Sûtra.

2 Volume; 6 Kiouen. Translated by Bôdhirutchi, of the Wei period.

Pou-sah-ying-lo-king.

Literally, the Neck-lace of Bôdhisatwa.

Translated by Buddhasmritti. 4 Volumes; 20 Kiouen. [It is a work of the advanced school, and highly mystical.]

Ta-fang-pien-fo-po-yen-king.

2 Volumes; 7 Kiouen. Translator's name lost.

Wou-sho-yeou-pou-sah-king.

The Sûtra of the Bôdhisatwa called Wou-sho-yeou ("without reliance;" or, "without aim.") 1 Volume; 4 Kiouen. Translated by Djnanakuta.

(a) San-mui-sz'-tao-kwang-hien-teng-i-king.

Anavatapta nagarâja paripritchch'a.

Translated by Dharmaraksha, of the Western Tsin dynasty.

(b) Ming-to-wou-shi-keou-ke-king.

Fifteen comparisons of certain subjects of discussion.

Translated by Ngan-shai-ko, of the Han dynasty.

(a) Ta-fang-kwang-un-hioh-sieou-to-lo-liu-i-king.

Mahâ vâipulya Sûtra râja *n.m y*. Sûtra. (?)

Translated by Buddhatara, of the Tang dynasty. 2 Parts.

(b) Fo-shwo-shi-teng-kung-te-king.

Pradîpadaniyâ Sûtra.

Translated by Nalandayasa, a Doctor of North India, during the Kao-Tsai period.

(c) Kiu-kong-san-mui-king.

Vâjra samâdhi Sûtra.

Translator's name lost.

Kwan-Fo-san-mui-hai-king.

Buddha samâdhi. (?)

2 Volumes; 10 Kiouen. Translated by Buddhabhadra, of the Eastern Tsin dynasty.

Pu-sah-pen-hing-king.

Incidents in the History of Bôdhisatwa.

Translator's name lost. 1 Volume; 3 Parts.

Ta-shing-mi-yen-king.

Ganavyûha Sutra.

Translated by Devakara, of the Tang dynasty. 1 Volume; 3 Parts.

(a) Ta-fa-ku-king.

The Drum of the Great Law.

Translated by Gunabhadra. 1 Volume; 2 Parts.

(b) Yue-shang-niu-king.

The Sutra called Yue-shang-niu (the woman above the Moon.)

Translated by Djnanakuta. 2 Parts.

Man-chu-sse-li-wen-king.

Manjusri paripritchch'a Sûtra.

Translated by Sanghapala 2 Parts.

Ju-lai-mi-yen-ts'ang-king.

Tathâgata garbha gunavyûha Sûtra. (?)

Translator's name lost. 2 Parts.

'An-kiu-mo-lo-hing.

Angulîmaliya Sûtra.

Translated by Gunabhadra. 4 Kiouen.

Pu-sah-nei-tsie-luh-po-lo-mi-king.

The modes in which Bodhisatwa practiced the paramitas, with a view to his own ultimate perfection.

Translated by a Shaman of the after Han dynasty.

Pu-sah-chi-shin-shi-ngo-hu-hi-tah.

The History of the Tower raised in the place where Bodhisatwa gave his body to feed the famished Tiger.

Translated by a Shaman of Turfan, called Dharma *pala* (?) of the North Liang dynasty.

XXVIII.

Yih-tseu-teng-lun-wang-king.

Ekachara ushnisha chakra râja Sûtra. (?)

Translated by Bodhirutchi, of the Tang dynasty. 2 Volumes; 6 Kiouen.

Hai-lung-wang-king.

Sagâranaga râja paripritchch'a Sûtra.

Translated by the Indian Dharmaraksha, of the Western Tsin dynasty. 1 Volume; 4 Kiouen.

Pa'o-leou-ko-pi-mi-to-lo-ni-king.

Mahâ mani vipula vimâna visva supratishthita guhyam paramarahasram kalpa raja nar dhârani. (*Julien, Concordance* 641.)

Translated by Bodirutchi, of the Tang dynasty. 1 Volume; 3 Parts.

Kin-kang-ting-yu-kia-nien-tung-king.

Vâjra sirsha guhya yoga Tantra. (?)

Translated by Vâjrajnana, of the Tang dynasty. 1 Volume; 4 Kiouen.

Tsi-fo-sho-shwo-shin-ch'au-king.

Sapta Buddha dhârani Sûtra. (?)

Translator's name lost. 1 Volume; 4 Kiouen.

Sou-po-ho-t'ong-tseu-king.

Subâhukumâra Sûtra.

1 Volume; 2 Parts. Translated by Yih-hing and another.

Ta-pi-lu-che-na-kia-che-king.

Mahavairochana dhârani Sûtra. (?)

Translated as before. 2 Volumes; 7 Kiouen.

Sou-sse-ti-kie-lo-king.

Susiddhikâra Sûtra. (*Vide Julien, Concordance* 542.)

Translated by Chakravara (?), of the Tang dynasty. 1 Volume; 4 Kiouen.

(*a*) Leou-cha-ho-lo-te-kwang-tai-tseu-king.

Rashtra gunaprâbha kumara Sûtra (but, *Vide Julien, Concordance* 735.)

Translated by Dharmaraksha, of the Western Tsin dynasty. pp. 25.

(*b*) Teih-chu-tien-tseu-sho-man-king.

The questions of a Heaven-born youth, Teih-chu. [Is this the Indraparipritchch Sutra? (*Concordance* 740).]

Ta-shing-sz'-fa-king.

Chaturshka nirhara *n.m.y.* Sûtra. *(Concordance* 588.*)*

Translated by Sikshananda, of the Tang dynasty. 1 Part; 10 pp.

Li-heou-hwui-pu-sa-sho-man-lai-Fo-fa-king.

The questionings of Bodhisatwa, called Li-heou-hwui.

Translated by a Shaman (called Nadi), of the Tang dynasty.

Pah-king.

Eight Sûtras.

1. Mau-chu-pa'o-ts'ang-to-lo-ni-king.

Ratnakarandaka vyuha *n.m.y.* Sûtra. *(Julien, Concordance* 802.*)*

Translated by Bodhirutchi, of the Tang dynasty. pp 23.

2. Seng-kia-ch'a-king.

Sangghata Sutra. (*Concordance* 517.)

Translated by the Son of the King of Udyana, named Upasena. 4 Kiouen.

3. Chuh-sing-po-ti-sin.

The birth of the heart of Bodhi.

Translated by Jnanakuta.

4. Fo-shwo-Fo-yin-san-mui-king.

Buddhamûdra Samadhi. (?)

Translated by 'An-shi-ko, of the after Han dynasty.

Fo-shwo-shi-i-teou-to-king.

Sramanadhuta Sûtra.

Translated by Gunabhadra.

Shu-ti-kia-king.

The History of a Nobleman called *Chudaka.*

Translated as above.

Fa-shang-chu-king.

The everlasting character of the Law.

Fo-shwo-shang-sheu-king.

The History of a King called 'Shang-sheu,' *i.e.*, long years.

[There are eight other volumes in this case, containing 78 short Sutras.]

XXIX.

Chung-A-han-king.

The Madyamagama, or Medium Agama.

Probably the same as the Majjhima Nikáya of the Southern Buddhists.

Translated by Gotamasanghadeva, of the Eastern Tsin dynasty. In 18 Volumes 60 Kiouen; and 18 Vaggas (*pin*); containing altogether 222 Sutras.

XXX.

Tsang-yih-A-han-king.

The numerical Agama, or literally, "Add-one-agama." The idea is taken from addin; *one* to every number after *ten*, in order to produce the next; so in this book one othe article is added to the preceding to make up the whole.

Translated by Dharmânanda, of the Fu-Tsin dynasty. 15 Volumes; 50 Kiouen.

XXXI.

Fo-shwo-chang-A-han-king.

The Dirghâgama Sûtra.

Translated by Buddhayasa and Buddhasmritti, of the Yaou-Tsin period (*circ* 410 A.D.) 7 Volumes; 22 Kiouen. [Deserves attention.]

Pie-i-tsa-a-han-king.

Selections from the Samyuktâgama Sûtra, according to another translation.

[Translator's name lost.] 6 Volumes; 18 Kiouen. Saktavargâgama Sûtra (?) (*Julien Concordance* 451).

(a) Tsa-a-han-king.

(b) Chang-a-han-shi-po-fa-king.

Abbreviated translations of the Samyuktâgama and the Dirghâgama. 1 Volume.

[Translator's name lost].

XXXII.

1. Sse-yan-tsze-san-tsang-chun.

[Ts'e-'en-sse-san-thsang-tch'ouen. *(Julien.)*]

This work is in three Parts or volumes, numbered *first*, *midale*, and *last*. (It includes *eight Kiouen*).

It is the original from which M. Julien translated his "Vie et voyages de Hiouen-Thsang." It is the work of "Hoèi-li, a Shaman of the Tang dynasty.

2. Shi-yih-king.

Eleven Sûtras.

This Book contains Eleven short Sutras, named as follows :—

(a) A-nan-man-sze-fuh-kih-heung-king.

Ananda asks Buddha respecting lucky and unlucky matters.

It was translated by Ngan-shai-ko, a Shaman of the after Hau dynasty, 220 A.D.

(b) Man-fa-king.

The Sûtra which treats of disregarding the Law.

This translation was made by Fa-k'hew (Torch of the Law), a Shaman of the Western Tsin dynasty, 265-313 A.D.

(c) A-nan-fen-pih-king.

The distinctions of Ananda.

Translated by a Shaman called Shing-kin, of the period *Kheih-fuh-Tsin* (date unknown.)

(d) Wu-moo-tseu-king.

Son of five Mothers.

Translated by a Upasikawa of the Woo Kingdom (*circ.* 180 A.D.) called Chi-kheen.

(e) Shah-mi-lo-king.

The Shamanera Sutra (The boy Samera.)

The Translator's name lost.

(f) Yu-ye-king.

The name of a Woman.

Translated by a Shaman of India, called Tan-wu-lan (Dharmalatsin), during the Eastern Tsin dynasty, 317-419 A.D.

(g) Yu-ye-niu-king.

The Sutra of the Woman called Yu-ye (another translation of the preceding.)

The name of the Translator is lost; but this work is named in the Catalogue of the Western Tsin dynasty, 265-313 A.D.

(h) O-suh-ta-king.

Asuta—apparently the name of a Woman—probably the same as the preceding Yu-ye.

Translated by Gunabhadra, an Indian (Priest), of the Sung dynasty (probably the Northern Sung, 420-477 A.D.)

(i) Mo-tang-niu-king.

The Story of the Matanga Woman.

This is the Story of the Matanga Woman and Ananda Her name is elsewhere given as Prakriti. The opening part bears some resemblance to the History of the Samaritan Woman at the Well.

Translated by 'Ngan-shai-ko, of the after Han dynasty, *circ.* 222 A.D.

(j) Mo-tang-niu-kiai-hing-chung-luh-sse-king.

Another translation of the preceding. Translator's name lost. Work is named in the Catalogue of the Western Tsin dynasty, 265-313 A.D.

(k) Mo-tang-kia-king (first part).

This is another translation of the preceding, in two Parts (Kiouen.)

Translated during the Woo dynasty (*circ.* 180 A.D.), by a Shaman named *" Liu-in, in conjunction with a Upasikwa called Chi-kheen.

(l) Second part of the above.

(l) is included with (k).

* Chu-liu-in. But I take *Chu* to mean "The Indian."

3. Hi-shai-in-pen-king.

The Sûtra which narrates the History of the Creation (first appearance of the World.)

Translated by Dharmakuta, of the Tsui dynasty, 589-619 A.D. The work is often quoted as the "In-pen" Sûtra. It is principally compiled from the work known as the Agama Sûtra.

4. Hi-shai-king.

The Book (Sûtra) of Genesis (the origin of the World.)

Translated by the same Priest as the preceding work.

5. Kwo-hai-in-tsai-in-kwo-king.

The Sutra which relates the present result (fruit) of past conduct.

This is a History of Buddha (Sukya Buddha.) It was translated by Gunabhadra, of the Sung dynasty (probably the Northern Sung dynasty), 420-477 A.D. It is in two Parts, comprising four Chapters (Kiouen.)

6. Fuh-shwo-Lau-tan-king.

Buddha relates the Pindadana Sûtra.

This is in one Part, and six Chapters. It was translated by two Priests of the Western Tsin dynasty, 265-313 A.D. They were named Fa-lai and Fa-kheu.

The Book, itself, is frequently quoted as the authority for the Mythological Stories of the Creation and Universe, as explained by Buddhists.

7. Shi-luh-king.

Sixteen Sûtras, under one cover.

The Sûtras are the following:—

(*a*) Chung-pen-hi-king.

This Sûtra, we are informed in a note, is extracted from the Dirghagama. It was translated by two Priests from India (Si-yu), in the after Han dynasty, *circ.* 220 A.D. Their names were Tan-kwo [Dharmaphala (?)] and Lai-mang. It is in two Parts, and contains, among other curious narratives, the History of the purchase of the Jatavana by Sudatta.

(*b*) Fuh-shwo-tsai-chi-king.

Buddha declares the seven species of Religious Knowledge.

This Sûtra was translated by a Priest, Chi-kheen, during the Woo dynasty. He is spoken of as belonging to the Yu-tchi (Getœ), *circ.* 180 A.D.

(c) **Fuh-shwo-han-shwui-u-king.**

Buddha declares the Salt-water comparison.

The Translator's name lost. The Sûtra is found in the Catalogue of the Western T dynasty, 265-313 A.D.

(d) **Fuh-shwo-yih-tsai-lau-shih-show-king.**

Translated by Ngan-shai-ko, a Shaman of the after Han dynasty, 220 A.D.

(e) **Fuh-shwo-yen-lo-wang-wu-tien-shi-tche-king.**

Buddha declares the five Heavenly Messengers of Jemma (Yamarâja).

Translated by Hwui-kan, a Priest of the Sung dynasty, 420 A.D.

(f) **Fuh-shwo-tih-shing-Ni-lai-king.**

Buddha declares the character of the Iron-Naraka-City, *i.e.*, the Avitchi Hell.

Translated by Dharmalatsin, a Shaman of the Eastern Tsin dynasty, 317-419 A.D.

(g) **Fuh-shwo-ku-lai-shai-shi-king.**

Buddha declares the character of past and future ages.

The Translator's name lost. The work, however, appears in the Catalogue of tl Eastern Tsin dynasty, 317-419 A.D.

(h) **Fuh-shwo-A-na-liu-pih-nien-king.**

Buddha declares the eight reflections of Aniruddha.

Translated by Chi-yaou, a Priest of the after Han dynasty, 220 A.D.

(i) **Fuh-shwo-li-shwuy-king.**

Buddha declares the Sûtra of "Removing Sleep" or "Drowsiness."

Translated by the Indian Fa-hu, Dharmaraksha, in the time of the Western Tsin dynasty, 265 A.D.

(j) **Fuh-shwo-shi-fa-fi-fa-king.**

Buddha discourses on the question of what is the Law (Religion), and what is not.

Translated by the Shaman, 'Ngan-shi-ko, in the after Han dynasty, 220 A.D.

(k) Fo-shwo-loh-siang-king.

Buddha discourses on the subject of "Thinking about Pleasure."

Translated by an Indian Shaman, called Fa-hu, in the Western Tsin dynasty, 265 A.]

(l) Fo-shwo-lo-fen-po-king.

Buddha declares the mode in which religious principles are undermined or destroyed.

Translated by a Priest of the after Han dynasty, called 'Ngan-shai-ko, 220 A.D.

(m) A'-now-pa-king.

Buddha discourses on the Anavatapta (Lake.) (?)

Translated by the Priest, Dharmalatsin, of the Eastern Tsin dynasty, 317-419 A.D.

(n) Fo-shwo-kau-yuh-king.

Buddha discourses on the search after pleasure.

Translated by the Shaman, Fa-kheu, of the Western Tsin dynasty, 265-313 A.D.

(o) Fo-shwo-sheu-shi-king.

Buddha discourses on the increase of years.

Translated by the Indian Priest, Fa-hu (Dharmaraksha), of the Western Tsin dynast, 265-313 A.D.

(p) Fo-shwo-Fan-chi-ke-shwui-tsing-king.

Buddha discourses on the subject of the Brahmachari, who estimated the purity of wate

The Translator's name lost. The work, however, occurs in the "Eastern Tsin" Inde 317-419 A.D.

8. Fo-shwo-sing-king.

This work is in two Volumes or Parts, and in five Chapters. It is a History of th Jâtakas of Buddha—in number, 55.

Translated by Fa-hu, of the Western Tsin dynasty, 265 A.D., 313 A.D. [It contain many curious Jâtakas.]

N.B.—"Sing," in the Title, probably for "Pen-sing."

9. Fo-shwo-nai-niu-khe-yu-yin-un-king.

(a) Buddha tells the History of the previous birth of the Woman, Khe-yu, of Benaras

Translated by 'Ngan-shai-ko, a Priest of the after Han dynasty, 220 A.D.

(*b*) **Fo-shwo-nai-niu-khe-po-king.**

Another translation of the previous work, by the same Translator.

10. Shi-tsai-king.

Seventeen Sûtras, named as follows :—

(*a*) **Fo-shwo-Fan-chi-o-pa-king.**

Buddha relates the History of the Brahmachari O-pa (Anavatapta (?).)

Translated by the Upasikawa Chi-kheen, of the Wu dynasty, a Yu-chi (Getœ), ci A.D. 180.

(*b*) **Fo-shwo-tsie-chi-kwo-king.**

Buddha declares the reward of quiet meditation or thought.

Translated by Dharmalatsin, a Shaman of the Eastern Tsin dynasty, 317-419 A.D.

(*c*) **Fo-shwo-pin-cha-ho-lo-king.**

Buddha relates the History of Pindavara. (?)

Translated by the Upasikawa Chi-kheen, of the Wu dynasty, belonging to the Yu-c (Getœ), *circ.* 190 A.D.

(*d*) **Fo-shwo-shen-sing-tseu-king.**

Buddha relates the History of Sujata pûtra.

Translated by a Shaman, Chi-fa-to, of the Western Tsin dynasty, 265-313 A.D.

(*e*) **Fo-shwo-Su-king.**

Buddha relates the History of (the Brahman) Su.

Translated by Fa-kheu, of the Western Tsin dynasty, 265-313 A.D.

(*f*) **Fo-shwo-fan-chi-o-po-lo-yan-man-tchung-tsun-king.**

Buddha recites the questioning of the Brahmachari O-po-lo-yan (Aparayana (?)) respecting the superiority of castes.

Translated by the Shaman, Dharmalatsin, of the Eastern Tsin dynasty, 317-419 A.D.

(*g*) **Fo-shwo-sse-ti-king.**

Buddha repeats the Sûtra of the four truths (Aryasatyani).

Translated by the Shaman, 'Ngan-shai-ko, of the after Han dynasty, 220 A.D.

(*h*) **Fo-shwo-heng-shwui-king.**

Buddha recites the Ganges-river Sûtra.

Translated by the Shaman, Fa-kheu, of the Western Tsin dynasty, 265 A.D.

(*i*) **Fo-shwo-chen-po-pi-kheu-king.**

Translated by Fa-kheu, 266 A.D.

(*j*) **Fo-shwo-pen-siang-e-chi-king.**

Buddha explains the fundamental relationships and connections of things.

By 'Ngan-shai-ko, 220 A.D.

(*k*) **Fo-shwo-un-pen-king.**

Buddha describes the connection of fundamental causes (Nidânas).

Translated by a Shaman of the Eastern Tsin dynasty, 317-419 A.D.

(*l*) **Fo-shwo-teng-sing-wang-ku-sse-king.**

Buddha relates the former History of the Head-born King (Murddha-jati (?).)

Translated by Fa-kheu, 265 A.D.

(*m*) **Fo-shwo-man-to-kih-wang-king.**

Buddha relates the History of the King Mandaha, or Mandaka.

Translated by Dharmalatsin, of the Northern Liang dynasty, *circ.* 260 A.D.

(*n*) **San-kwai-wu-kiai-tsse-sin-to-li-kung-tih-king.**

Buddha relates various degrees of merit attaching to the progressive religious profession.

Translator's name lost. Belongs to the Eastern Tsin, 317 A.D.

(*o*) **Fo-shwo-Su-ta-king.**

The History of Sudatta, or Suda.

Translated by Kunavata, of the Seou-Tse dynasty [the Tse dynasty founded by Seou-Taouching (Seou, or Seaou, being the Duke of Tse)], *circ.* 480 A.D.

(p) **Fo-wei-hwang-chuh-un-lo-po-lo-men-shwo-hioh-king.**

Buddha recites the Sûtra of Bôdhi, or true wisdom, for the sake of a Brahman, call Yellow-bamboo-garden (hwang-chuh-un).

Translator's name lost.

(q) **Fo-shwo-fan-mo-u-king.**

Buddha relates the Brahma comparison.

Translated by Chi-kheen, of the Wu dynasty, *circ.* 190 A.D.

11. 'Rh-shi-king.

Twenty Sûtras, in one case, as follows :—

(a) **Fo-shwo-fuh-yin-king.**

Buddha declares the method of overcoming lust.

Translated by a Shaman, Fa-kheu, of the Western Tsin dynasty, 220 A.D.

(b) **Fo-shwo-Mo-in-lu-king.**

Buddha recites the jealousy and distraction caused by Mara (the Devil).

The Translator's name lost The Book, however, is named in the Catalogue of th after Han dynasty, 220 A.D.

(c) **Fo-shwo-Pe-mo-she-mo-lin-king.**

Buddha relates the Story of Mogalan's temptation by the wicked Mara.

Translated by Chi-kheen, a Upasikawa of the Wu dynasty, belonging to the Yu-ch (Getœ), *circ.* 190 A.D.

(d) **Fo-shwo-ni-lai-king.**

Buddha explains the character of the different Narakas (Hells.)

Translated by the Priest, Dharmara, of the Eastern Tsin dynasty, 330 A.D.

(e) **Fo-shwo-yau-po-i-Tho-she-ka-king.**

Buddha relates the History of the Upasiká Tho-she-ka (Dvashka (?).)

The Translator's name lost. The Book, however, is named in the Index of the Sung dynasty, 420 (?), or 800 (?) A.D.

(*f*) **Fo-shwo-chai-king.**

Buddha recites the Rules of Fasting.

By Chi-kheen, of the Wu dynasty, 180 A.D.

(*g*) **Fo-shwo-fu-yin-king.**

Buddha relates the Sûtra which explains Grief or Sorrow.

Translated during the after Han dynasty, 220 A.D.

(*h*) **Fo-shwo-fu-yin-in-sze-king.**

Buddha discourses on the causes of Sorrow (Dukha.)

Translated by Fa-kheu, of the Western Tsin dynasty, 265-313 A.D.

(*i*) **Fo-shwo-shi-mo-nan-pen-king.**

Buddha recites the previous History of the Sakya, Mo-nan.

Translated by Chi-kheen, of the Wu State, *circ.* 180 A.D., belonging to the Getœ.

(*j*) **Fo-shwo-hea-mo-suh-king.**

Buddha relates the History of Hea-mo-suh.

Translated by Gunabhadra, of the Sung dynasty.

(*k*) **Fo-shwo-po-lo-men-tseu-ming-tchung-ui-nien-puh-li-king.**

Buddha relates the History of the Brahmanaputra who, at the end of life, could put away libidinous thoughts.

Translated by 'Ngan-shai-ko, of the after Han dynasty, 220 A.D.

(*l*) **Fo-shwo-shi-chi-ku-sse-pih-shing-yin-king.**

Buddha relates the History of the House-holder Shi-chi.

Translated by 'Ngan-shai-ko, of the after Han dynasty, 220 A.D.

(*m*) **Fo-shwo-ts'e-kin-king.**

Buddha discourses on Heresy.

Translator's name lost. The Book named in the Sung Catalogue or Index.

(n) Fo-shwo-tsien-u-king.

Buddha relates the Arrow-parable, or comparison.

Translator's name lost. The Book found in the Index of the Eastern Tsin, 360 A.D.

(o) Fo-shwo-pho-fa-i-king.

Buddha relates the principle or truth of the wide-spreading or universal Dharma.

Translated by 'Ngan-shai-ko, of the after Han dynasty, 220 A D.

(p) Fo-shwo-kwang-i-fa-men-king.

Buddha declares the religious principle of extensive or wide significance.

[This is taken from the first Section *(Vagga)* of the Middle Agama.]

Translated by Chun-ti, a Priest of the Chin dynasty, 557-583 A.D.

(q) Fo-shwo-kiai-tih-hiang-king.

Buddha speaks upon the fragrance of Moral Excellency.

Translated by Dharmalatsin, a Priest of the Eastern dynasty, 317-419 A.D.

(r) Fo-shwo-sse-yin-chuh-in-shai-kan-king.

Buddha tells the History of four Men who went out to see the World.

Translated by Gunabhadra, of the Sung dynasty.

(s) Fo-shwo-chu-fa-pen-king.

Buddha speaks on the origin of all Laws (or, *systems* or *things.*)

Translated by Chi-kheen, a Upasikawa of the Wu dynasty, 180 A.D.

(t) Fo-shwo-kiu-tan-mi-ki-kwo-king.

Buddha declares the antecedent History of Gotami.

Translated by Chi-kheen, of the Wu dynasty, 180 A.D.

12. She-tau-keen-king.

The Sardula Karna Sûtra.

This is the History of Prakriti, the Matanga Woman, as given in Burnouf (Introduction to Indian Buddhism), p. 206, n.

Translated by Tchu-fa-hu, of the Western Tsin dynasty, 265 A.D. [This translation agrees with Burnouf's, and was evidently made from the Pali or Prakrit.]

13. Che-chan-ping-pe-iu-king.

Secret methods of overcoming that which interferes with the contemplation (of asceti in the forest.)

This Sûtra was delivered on the occasion of an Elephant Fight, which some of t young Sâkyas got up in the neighbourhood of the Jatavana, thereby disturbing t religious ecstasy of some of the occupants of the Monastery.

Translated by Ping-sheng, of the North Liang dynasty. In two Parts.

14. (a) Kwei-man-muh-lin-king.

A Demon asks Mogalan certain questions.

Translated by 'Ngan-shai-ko, of the after Han dynasty, 220 A.D.

(b) Tsah-tsong-king.

Various Secrets.

Appears to be the same as the preceding. It gives an account of questions asked various Demons on the banks of the Ganges, and the answers of Mogalan, as to t cause of their sufferings.

Translated by Fa-hien, of the Eastern Tsin dynasty, 317-419 A.D.

(c) 'Ngo-kwei-po-ying-king.

The Retribution received by various Pretas.

This is another version of the above. The Translator's name lost. Appears in t Catalogue of the Eastern Tsin *(supra.)*

(d) Fo-shwo-sz-shi-i-cheung-king.

The Sûtra of Forty-two Sections.

Translated by Kasyapa Matanga, in conjunction with Chu-fa-lan (the Indian Dharmar -(ksha) (?)), during the after Han dynasty, 220 A.D.

But, as Chu-fa-lan and his co-adjutors lined under the Eastern Han dynasty, vi 63 A.D., it is probable that all the preceding dates, which reckon under the "After Har dynasty, are to be referred to the earlier line of the Eastern Hans, viz., about (A.D., to 190 A.D.

15. I-shi-luh-king.

Twenty-six Sûtras, of which the following is a list :—

(a) Fo-shwo-Tsun-shang-king.

Buddha relates the History of the Heavenly Messenger.

Translated by Chu-fa-hu, a Priest of the Western Tsin dynasty, 265-313 A.D.

(b) Fo-shwo-Ying-woo-king.

The Parrot Sûtra.

Translated by Gunabhadra, of the Lew-Sung dynasty.

This Sûtra was spoken in the Jatavana Vihara, at Sravasti. [There is a curious phr which occurs in this and other Sûtras, viz , *Fen-wei*, " Divide the Streets," in the ser of " Going a Begging "] This Sûtra appears to be a History of a certain House-hol in Sravasti, called " Ying-woo," whose Dog interrupted Sakya as he was begging.

This Sûtra comprises 10 double pp.

(c) Fo-shwo-tow-theou-king.

Buddha declares the Devadatta (?) Sutra.

This appears to be another translation of the preceding. It relates the History of t Brahman whose Dog attacked Buddha whilst begging in Sravasti.

The Translator's name lost. But the Title of the work is found in the Catalogue the Western Tsin dynasty, 220 A D. 4 pp.; 1 Part.

(d) Fo-shwo-i-king.

Buddha declares (or explains) the thoughts (of certain Bhikshus.)

This Sutra was delivered in Sravasti, on the occasion of various Bhikshus coming Buddha and asking for an explanation of their thoughts.

Translated by Fa-hu, of the Western Tsin dynasty, 220 A.D. pp. 3.

(e) Fo-shwo-Ying-fa-king.

Buddha declares the right (or, proper) Law.

Delivered at Sravasti, for the sake of the Bhikshus.

Translated by Chu-fa-hu, of the Western Tsin dynasty. Includes 4 pp.

(f) Fo-shwo-po-sze-nih wong-ta-hu-pang-to-fen-shun-king.

Buddha recites the Sutra of the burial of the Queen of Prasenajit.

Translated by Fa-kheu, of the Western Tsin dynasty, 220 A.D. 3 pp.

(g) Su-mo-ti-niu-king.

The Sutra that relates the history of Samati (the daughter of Anathapindada.)

Delivered at Sravasti, in the presence of all the Bhikshus. 19 pp.

Translated by the Upasikawa, Chi-kheen of the Wu dynasty, belonging to the Yu-ch

(g) Fo-shwo-san-mo-kih-king.

This seems to be another translation of the former Sûtra. The author's name is Liu-in, of the Wu dynasty, 180 A.D. pp. 9.

(h) Fo-shwo-po-lo-men-pe-sse-king.

Buddha relates the Sûtra about "Avoiding Death."

[Five Brahmans consider how they may avoid death *e.g.r.*, by transporting themselves into the sea, into space, &c.]

Translated by 'Ngan-shai-ko, of the after Han dynasty. pp. 3.

(i) Pin-pi-sha-lo-wang-chi-Fo-kung-yeung-king.

The invitation given by Bimbasara râja to Buddha.

Translated by Fa-kheu, a Shaman of the Western Tsin dynasty, 180 A.D. pp. 5.

(j) Fo-shwo-chang-che-tseu-luh-kwo-chuh-kia-king.

Buddha recites the History of 'Luh-kwo,' the Son of a Nobleman (Grihapati), and how he became a disciple.

Translated by Hwui-kan, a Priest of the Sung dynasty. pp. 3.

(k) Fo-shwo-Yang-ku-ma-king.

The Angulimâlya Sûtra.

Delivered at Sravasti. pp. 7. Translated by Chu-fa-hu, of the Sung dynasty.

(l) Fo-shwo-Yang-ku-wan-king.

The Angulimâlya Sûtra.

Another version, by a Priest of the Western Tsin dynasty, but of the same name as the former—Chu-fa-hu. pp. 7.

(m) Fo-shwo-lih-sse-e-shan-king.

Buddha recites the History of the Malla (or, Citizen of Vaisali), who tried to move or transplant a Mountain.

Translated by Fa-hu, of the Western Tsin dynasty. pp. 5.

(n) Fo-shwo-sz'-mi-tsang-yeou-fa-king.

Buddha declares the four miraculous signs of a Chakravartin, or Universal Monarch.

Translated by Fa-hu, of the Western Tsin dynasty. pp. 2.

(o) Fo-shwo-shi-li-fu-mu-kin-lin-yaou-sz'-kheu-king.

Buddha recites the History of Sariputra and Mogalan going through the four road (*i.e.*, the different Kingdoms, or the World), a-begging. pp. 3.

Translated by Mang-tseang, of the after Han dynasty, 63 A.D.

[The following nine Sutras are said to be under the same original envelope or cover.]

(p) Tse-fuh-fu-moo-sing-tsze-king.

The sur-names and names of the Fathers and Mothers of the seven Buddhas.

Translated by an unknown author belonging to the Tsaou-Wei period. pp. 4.

(q) Fo-shwo-fang-'ngau-king.

Buddha recites the History of Fang-'ngau (liberating the Ox.)

Translated by Kumarajiva, a Priest of the Yaou-Tsin dynasty, 420 A.D. pp. 5.

(r) Un-hi-king.

The Sutra which explains the first rising of life (Nidanas.)

Translated by Hiouen Thsang, of the Tang dynasty. pp. 3.

(s) Fo-shwo-shi-i-siang-sze-nien-ju-lai-king.

Buddha recites eleven methods in which we ought to reflect upon the persoı of Tathâgata.

Translated by Gunabhadra, a Priest of the Sung dynasty.

(t) Fo-shwo-sz-ni-lai-king.

Buddha speaks upon the four Hells (Narakas.)

Translated by the Indian Priest, Dharmara (ksha), of the Eastern Tsin dynasty, *circ* 300 A.D.

(u) She-wei-kwo-wang-mang-kin-shi-sze-king.

The King of Sravasti dreams of ten different things.

The Translator's name lost. The Book appears in the Western Tsin Catalogue, 220 A.D

(v) Fo-shwo-kwo-wang-puh-lai-sien-ni-shi-mong-king.

The ten dreams of Prasenajit, the Maharaja (King of the Country.)

Translated by Dharmalatsin, of the Eastern Tsin dynasty, 300 A.D. pp. 6.

(w) A-nan-tung-hioh-king.

The History of the fellow-student, or religious companion of Ananda.

Translated by 'Ngan-shai-ko, of the after Han dynasty, 62 A.D. pp. 4.

(*x*) **Wu-wan-kiai-hung-king.**

The emptiness of the five skhandas.

Translated by I-tsing, of the Tang dynasty. pp. 2.

(*y*) **A-nan-tung-hioh-king.**

The Sûtra of the fellow-learner of Ananda (Gupta a Bhikshu of Sravasti, and a fell student or learner with Ananda).

Translated by 'Ngan-shai-ko, of the after Han dynasty.

16. Shi-luh-king.

Sixteen Sûtras, as follows :—

(*a*) **Fo-shwo-tsah-chu-san-kwan-king.**

Buddha delivers the Sûtra of the Seven places (Ayatanas) and the Three subjects contemplation (Kwan).

Translated by 'Ngan-shai-ko, of the after Han dynasty. In 2 Parts; pp. 28.

(*b*) **A-na-pin-te-fa-tsih-tseu-king.**

Account of the conversion of Seven Children of A-na-pin-te (Anathapindada.)

Translated by 'Ngan-shai-ko, of the after Han dynasty. pp. 5.

(*c*) **Fo-shwo-tai-'ai-tau-pan-ni-pan.**

Buddha gives an account of the Nirvâna of Mahâprajapati.

Translated bs Pih-fa-tsu of the Western Tsin dynasty, 265 A.D. pp. 8

(*d*) **Fo-moo-pan-ni-pan-king.**

The Nirvâna of the Mother of Buddha.

Translated by Shi-hwui-kan, of the Sung dynasty. pp. 5.

(*e*) **Fo-shwo-shing-fa-yin-king.**

Buddha declares the Seal of the Holy Law.

Translated by Chu-fa-hu, a Priest of the Western Tsin dynasty, 265 A.D. pp. 2.

(*f*) **Fo-shwo-shwui-mo-sho-leih-king.**

Buddha discourses on the Froth and Bubbles of the River Ganges.

Translated by Dharmalatsin, of the Eastern Tsin dynasty, 330 A.D. pp. 3.

(g) Fo-shwo-puh-sze-shan-i-king.

Buddha discourses on the want of guarding the thoughts in any individual.

Translated by the Upasikawa Chi-kheen, of the Wu dynasty, 190 A.D., belonging to the Yu-chi (Getœ). p. 1.

(h) Fo-shwo-mun-un-tseu-king.

Buddha relates the History of the Child Mun-un.

Translator's name lost. In the Catalogue of the Eastern Tsin dynasty. pp. 3.

(i) Chun-fa-lun.

Turning the Wheel of the Law.

Translated by 'Ngan-shai-ko, of the after Han dynasty. pp. 3.

(j) Fo-shwo-san-chun-fa-Lun-king.

Buddha repeats the thrice-turned Wheel of the Law.

Translated by I-tsing, of the Tang dynasty. pp. 3.

(k) Fo-shwo-pah-tching-tan-king.

Buddha declares the Eight kinds of true Wisdom, or Religious Profession.

Translated by 'Ngan-shai-ko, of the after Han dynasty. pp. 2.

(l) Nan-ti-shi-king.

History of Nanda, or Nandi, the Sâkya.

Translated by Fa-kheu, of the Western Tsin dynasty, 220 A.D. pp. 4.

(m) Fo-shwo-ma-yeou-san-siang-king.

Buddha relates the three marks of the good horse.

Translated by Chi-yaou of the after Han dynasty. pp. 2.

(n) Fo-shwo-ma-yeou-pah-thae-pi-yin-king.

Buddha speaks of the eight points of resemblance between man and the horse.

Translated by Chi-yaou, of the after Han dynasty. pp. 2.

(o) Fo-shwo-siang-ying-siang-ho-king.

Buddha recites the Sûtra relating to what ought to be practiced by the Bhikshus, and what ought not, in their relationship as associates.

Translated by Fa-kheu, of the Western Tsin dynasty, 260 A.D. pp. 2.

XXXIII.

This case contains fourteen volumes, including seventy four chapters (Kiouen.)

The whole is occupied by a work called *Tching-fa-nien-chu-king*, which may be translated " Memorable passages of the True Law." It is probably the same work as that quoted in the South as " *Saddharma ppakisini.*"

The following is a synopsis of contents—The First ch'hih includes five chapters in which are discussed—

1. The ten superior or happy ways of birth.

2. The question of Life and Death.

The Second and Third ch'hih include Ten Chapters (Kiouen), subject discussed throughout—

1. The different Hells.

The Fourth ch'hih contains Six Chapters, subject discussed—

1. The condition of the Pretas ('Ngo-kwei)

2. The Birth as a Beast.

The next Nine ch'hih, viz., from Five to Thirteen, are occupied throughout Forty-two Chapters in discussing—

1. The character of Heaven, or the Heavens.

The Fourteenth ch'hih, comprising Seven Chapters, is occupied by the following subject—

1. Memorable passages or considerations about the Human Body.

The whole of this work is interesting, as it contains a full account of the Buddhist Kosmos. It was translated into Chinese by a Brahman, called Gotama Prajnaruchi, during the time of the Youen Wei, one of the three contending States, 200 A.D.

XXXVI.

Fo-pen-hing-tsi-king.

According to *Wassilief* this is a Chinese Version of the Abinishkramana Sûtra. *Stas. Julien* speaks of it (*Concordance* 167) as a version of the *Budaha tcharitra.*

Translated by Djnanakuta (*Julien* prefers Djnanagupta). In 60 kiouen.

XXXV.

1. Sheou-hu-ta-tsien-kwo-t'u-king.

Mahâ sahasra mandala Sûtra.

1 Volume; 2 Parts. Translated during the Sung dynasty, by Shi-hu. It is a Book of dharânis.

2. Miau-fa-shing-nien-chu-king.

Probably of the same character as the "Tching-fa-nien-chu-king" *(Concordance* 694) only the present work is in 8 Volumes, whereas that is in 70.

Translated by Fa-tien, a Priest of the Sung dynasty.

3. Ta-p'ao-tsi-ching-fa-king.

Mahakasyapa paripritchch'a *n.m.y.* Sûtra *(Concordance* 623.)

1 Volume; 5 Parts. Translated by Shi-hu, of the Sung dynasty.

4. Ta-fang-kwang-tsung-chi-p'ao-kwong-ming-king.

A Sûtra delivered on the Gridhrakuta Hill, near Rajagriha, and translated by Fa-tien of the Sung dynasty. 1 Volume; 5 Chapters.

5. (*a*) Yin-chi-yih-king.

(*b*) Fo-shwo in-un-sang-hu-king.

Two Sûtras in one volume; the latter is the same as the Sangha rakshita Avadâna translated by Burnouf (*Introduction* 313, ss)

The first dates from the after Han dynasty, translated by 'Ngan-shai-ko; the secon has no translator's name given.

Shi-tsah-king.

Seventeen short Sûtras, in one Volume.

The third of these is the Story of the Man who was ploughing with his Son in th field, and on the sudden death of the latter, the Father delayed not in his work, but sent message home to prepare dinner only for one, instead of two; his Mother, Sister, Wif and Servant, also exhibited the same indifference, regarding death as a necessity, an possibly a subject for joy, rather than sorrow.

Most of these Sûtras were translated during the early Sung dynasty.

[There are more than 100 other short Sutras in this case, in Eight Volumes, all c which deserve some examination.]

XXXVI.

1. Ta-mo-li-chi-Pu-sah-king.

The Sutra of the Bôhisatwa Maritchi, in Two Volumes, comprising Seven Chapters.

Translated by a Priest (Ta-sse) of Tien-sih, called Tsai-fung, during the Sung dynast It contains the dharani used in the worship of Maritchi.

2. Chung-hu-mo-ho-ti-king.

This would appear to be a copy of the Mahâvastu, according to the version of th Mahasanghikas. It contains a History of Sâkya Buddha, from the time of the origin c the world. It is in 2 Volumes, and comprises 13 Chapters or Kiouen.

Translated by Fa-kien, a Priest of the Sung dynasty.

3. Fo-shwo-chuh-sing-san-fa-tsong-king.

The Mother of Buddha (Maha Prajna) produces, or brings forth, the three-folc Law Treasure.

This is a work of the Prajna Parimita class. In 4 Volumes, including 25 Chapters o Kiouen. It was translated by Shi-hu and others, of the Sung dynasty.

4. Ta-fang-kwong-Shen-hau-fong-pien-king.

The expanded Sûtra relating to the expedients used by the Bôdhisatwa Shen-hau (or, i may be, the illustrious expedients used by the Bôdhisatwa) in the conversion of men.

A Sûtra of the Vaipulya class. In 1 Volume and 4 Chapters. Translated by Shi-hu of the Sung dynasty.

5. Wu-king-tung-pen.

Five Sûtras, translated from one original (work, or MS.) [all contain Dhâranis.]

6. (*a*) Tai-shing-puh-sze-i-shin-tung-keng-kiai-king.

Buddha delivers the Sûtra called the infinite and incomprehensibly-bounded Universe.

Translated by Shi-hu, of the Sung dynasty. Spoken in the Palace of the Bôdhisatw: Kwong-ming, for the sake of Nâgas and others. Two parts. 32 double pp.

(*b*) Fo-shwo-kih-ku-chang-tche-niu-teh-to-yin-un-king.

Buddha recites the causes that led to the salvation (deliverance) of the wife of the Nobleman Kih-ku (Anathapindada)

Delivered in the Jetavana at Sravasti. (This is the story of Anathapindada's daughte and the heretics.) In 3 parts; 30 double pp. Translated by Shi-hu, of the Sung dynasty

(*c*) Fo-shwo-tai-tsah-fa-men-king.

Buddha delivers the Sutra which treats of the great concourse of methods of Salvation.

Delivered at Vaisali, for the sake of some Bhikshus who quarrelled with the Nirgran thas and others. pp. 25. [Translated as before.]

[The three Sutras preceding, are in one Volume, and are therefore numbered *a*, *b*, *c*.]

7. Pah-king.

Eight Sutras, named as follows :—

(*a*) Fo-shwo-kuh-teng-i-king.

Buddha declares the Categories of Fixed Truths.

(This is an account of the various Categories of Buddhist Philosophy,—such as the five skandha, the eighteen worlds (bhuvas), the 12 ayatanas, and so on.)

Delivered at Sravasti, for the sake of the Bhikshus. pp. 12. Translated by Fa-kien, of the Sung dynasty.

(b) **Fo-shwo-u-kwoh-king.**

Buddha relates the History of U-kwoh (defend country.)

Delivered in the Village of Tara (To-lo), for the sake of the congregation of Bhikshus and others. pp. 10. [Same Translator.]

(c) **Fo-shwo-fen-pih-pu-shi-king.**

Buddha distinguishes the various kinds of charitable gifts, especially of garments: occasioned by an offering made by the Bhikshuni Mahâprajapati. pp. 4. Translated by Shi-hu (as before.)

(d) **Fo-shwo fen-pih-un-sing-king.**

This was spoken at Uravilva, for the sake of Maha Brahma. It is an account of the Nidanas, or causes of existence. pp. 7. Translated by Shi-hu.

(e) **Fo-shwo-fa-yin-king.**

Buddha declares the Seal of the Law.

Delivered at Sravasti, for the sake of the Bhikshus. pp. 2. [Translated as before.]

(f) **Fo-shwo-tai-sing-i-king.**

Buddha relates the principle of Birth (or, reason of Birth, *i.e.*, continued Birth.)

Delivered at Uravilva, for the sake of Ananda. pp. 8. [Translated as before.]

(g) **Fo-shwo-fa-Po-ti-sin-po-tchu-Mo-king.**

Buddha delivers the method of arriving at the Heart of Bôdhi,—and thus overcoming all the Evil Ones (Devils.)

Delivered in the Kalandavenuvana, at Râjagriha, for the sake of all the Bhikshus. 19 pp. [Translated as before.]

(h) **Fo-shwo-shing-fuh-moo-pan-jo-po-lo-mi-king.**

Buddha delivers the Prajnaparamita of the Holy Mother of Buddha (*i.e.*, Maha prajna).

Delivered on the Vulture Peak, near Râjagriha. pp. 2. [Translated as before.]

8. Kiu-king-tung-pun.

Nine Sûtras, included in one case or original packet.

(a) Two Sûtras, in one Chapter or Kiouen.

1. Fo-shwo-mi-li-chi-ti-po-fa-wan-king.

Buddha declares the Sûtra of the Flowery Chaplet of Maritchi Devî.

Translated by *Puh-hung* (Amogha), of the Tang dynasty. pp. 14.

8. Fo-shwo-mo-li-chi-Tien-king.

Buddha declares the Sûtra of Maritchi Devî.

Translated by the same writer. pp. 5.

Fo-shwo-Mo-li-chi-tien-to-lo-li-chau-king.

Buddha recites the Dhârani of Maritchi Devî.

Translated by an unknown writer. pp. 2.

(c) Fo-shwo-chang-tche-shi-po-king.

Buddha recites the Sûtra of the reward of charity, for the benefit of the Nobleman Anathapindada.

Translated by Fa-tien, of the Sung dynasty. pp. 8.

(d) Fo-shwo-pi-sha-men-Tien-wang-king.

Buddha recites the Sûtra of the Devarâja Vaisravana.

Translated by Fa-tien, of the Sung dynasty. pp. 9.

(e) Pi-po-she-Fo-king.

The Sutra of Vibhasi Buddha.

Translated by Fa-tien, of the Sung dynasty. Part 1; pp. 8. Part 2; pp. 9.

(f) San-king-tung-kiouen.

Three Sûtras, in one Chapter [on Samadhi.]

9. Fo-shwo-kiai-hia-king.

Buddha recites the Sûtra called "Release, or explain, Summer." [This appears to be the Title of a Sûtra delivered during the Summer Retreat, or the season of the Rains (Varshas).]

Translated by Fa-khin (Dharmabhadra), of the Sung dynasty. pp. 4.

10. (a) Fo-shwo-ti-shi-sho-man-king.

Buddha relates the Sûtra of the questions of Sâkrarâja.

Translated as before. pp. 14.

(b) Fo-shwo-mi-tsang-yeou-ching-fa-king.

Buddha recites the Sûtra called the True Law (Saddharma,) of things which never yet happened (naturally.) [In other words, the Sutra of Miracles, or *adbhuta dharma* or *ardbhuta saddharma.*]

Translated by Fa-tien, of the Sung dynasty. Chapter 1; pp. 12. Chapter 2; pp. 8 Chapter 3, pp. 14. Chapter 4; pp. 12. Chapter; 5 pp. 11. Chapter 6; pp. 13.

11. (*a*) **Fo-moo-pao-tih-tsong-pan-jo-po-lo-mi-king.**

The Prajna Paramita Sûtra of the Mother of Buddha.

Translated by Fa-khin, of the Sung dynasty. In 3 Parts; pp. 34.

(*b*) **Fo-shwo-ti-shi-pan-jo-po-lo-mi-to-sin-king.**

Buddha recites the Sûtra called the Heart of the Prajna Paramita of Sakraraja.

Translated by Shi-hu, of the Sung dynasty. pp. 5.

(*c*) **Fo-shwo-tchu-Fo-king.**

Buddha recites the Sûtra called "All the Buddhas."

Translated by Shi-hu (as before.) pp. 2.

(*d*) **Ta-shing-she-li-sha-tan-mo-king.**

Mahayana Sirsha dharma Sûtra. (?)

Translated by Shi-hu, of the Sung dynasty. pp. 7.

(*e*) **Fo-shwo-ta-kong-hiang-to-lo-ni-king.**

Buddha recites the Sûtra called *Maha vajra ghanda dharani*.

Translated as before. pp. 3.

12. Shi-wu-king-tung-pen.

Fifteen Sûtras, the same copy or original, as follows:—

(*a*) **Tsui-shang-ta-shing-kin-kong-ta-kiau-pao-wang-king.**

This Sûtra only admits of the following literal translation: "The highest-great-vehicle, diamond-great-doctrine, precious-king Sutra."

Translated by Fa-tien, of the Sung dynasty. Cap. 1; pp. 10. Cap. 2; pp. 12.

(*b*) **Fo-shwo-sah-pah-to-hi-pi-yu-nai-ye.**

Buddha recites the Sutra of every kind of Miracle (Sarvata ardbhutaya (?).)

Translated by Fa-kien, of the Sung dynasty. pp. 13.

(*c*) **Po-tai-sin-kwan-shi.**

The Heart of Bôdhi beholding or contemplating Sâkya.

Translated by Fa-tien, of the Sung dynasty. pp. 3.

(*d*) **Fo-shwo-hu-kwo-tsun-tche-sho-man-tai-shing-king.**

The questions of 'Hu-kwo' (Lokapalita), a Sutra of the Great Vehicle. In 4 Caps.; pp. 32.

(e) **Fo-shwo-sz-wu-sho-wai-king.**

Buddha recites the Sûtra called "the four fearless dispositions or distinctions."

Translated by Shi-hu, of the Sung dynasty, pp. 2.

[The remaining contain Dhârani.]

13. Shi-kiu-king.

Nineteen Sutras (of no importance.)

14. I-shi-king-tung-pen.

Twenty Sûtras (of which the following are the most important.)

(a) **Fo-shwo-A-lo-han-kiu-tih-king.**

Buddha recounts the numerous virtues (or religious qualifications) of the Rahat.

Delivered at Sravasti in the Jetavana, and translated into Chinese by Fa-kien, of the Sung dynasty. pp. 12.

(b) **Fo-shwo-pah-tai-ling-tah-ming-ho.**

Buddha recites the names of eight great sacred places. (The words *ling-tah*, may simply mean "Religious buildings," *i.e.*, "Chaityas.")

No place named. Translated by Fa-kien, of the Sung dynasty.

The sacred spots are these—1. The Lumbini garden, at Kapilavastu, where Buddha was born. 2. The bank of the Nairanjana River in Maghada, underneath the tree where Buddha attained perfect enlightenment. 3. The place near Benares where Buddha first turned the wheel of the Law, *i.e.*, began to preach. 4. The Jetavana, near Sravasti where Buddha exhibited great spiritual manifestations. 5. The city of the hump-backed woman,* where Buddha descended from the Trayastrinshas Heaven. 6. The city of Râjagrihâ, in the place where, after a division among the Priests, Buddha made many conversions by his preaching. 7. The city of Kwang-yan (wide-splendor), in the sacred spot where (Buddha) considered and reflected on the length of (his) years. 8. The Sal Grove at Kusinagara, where Buddha attained Nirvana.

[There is a further account, forming part of the Sutra, of the different places in which Buddha passed his life, and the length of time he resided in each.]

Translated as before. pp. 3.

(c) **Fo-shwo-pin-po-sha-lo-wang-king.**

Buddha recites the Sutra known as Bimbasara râja.

Delivered at Rajagriha. Translated as before. pp. 7.

(d) **Fo-shwo-yin-sien-king.**

Buddha declares the Sutra called Yin-sien (Man-Rishi.)

Delivered in a Vihara called Kwan-tso-kia, near the city of Na-ti-kia. Translated as before. pp. 12.

---

* Canoj.

(e) **Fo-shwo-kan-shing-u-king.**

Buddha recites the parable of the old-city.

Delivered at Sravasti, in the Jetavana, and translated as before. pp. 6.

(*f*) **Fo-shwo-sin-kiai-chi-lih-king.**

Buddha speaks on the power of faith, as a means of deliverance; and also on the efficacy of Wisdom.

Delivered at Sravasti. in the Jetavana, and translated as before. pp. 7.

15. (*a*) **Tsah-Fo-king.**

Buddha declares the Sutra called "The Seven Buddhas" [Sapta Buddhaka Sutra (?).]

Delivered at Sravasti. Translated by Fa-tien, of the Sung dynasty. pp. 15.

[Contains a History of the Seven Manushi Buddhas.]

(*b*) **Fo-shwo-kiai-gae-king.**

Buddha declares the Sutra that relates to freedom from, or deliverance from, the power of Love (Lust.)

Delivered at Sravasti. Translated by Fa-tien, of the Sung dynasty. pp. 4.

(*c*) **Fo-shwo-pien-chiu-pan-jo-po-lo-mi-to-king.**

Buddha recites the History of the widely glorious Prajna Paramita.

Translated by Shi-hu, of the Sung dynasty. pp. 9.

(*d*) **Fo-shwo-ta-shing-wu-liang-shau-chwong-yan-king.**

Buddha recites the Sutra called the glorious never ending (infinite years) (Sutra) of the Great Vehicle.

Delivered on the Vulture Peak, near Rajagriha. Translated by Fa-kien, of the Sung dynasty. In 3 Parts; pp. 30.

16. Tsah-king-tung-pen.

Seven Sutras (of no importance.)

XXXVII.

1. Pah-king.

Eight Sutras, named thus—

(*a*) **Fo-shwo-wu-wai-shau-sho-man-ta-shing-king.**

Buddha declares the Sutra belonging to the Great Vehicle, which relates the questions of the (Nobleman) Wu-wai-shan.

Delivered at Sravasti. Translated by Shi-hu, of the Sung dynasty. pp. 17.

(b) Fo-shwo-yue-u-king.

The parable or comparison of the Moon.

Delivered in the Kalandavenuvana, near Râjagriha. Translated by Shi-hu, of the Su dynasty. pp. 3.

(c) Fo-shwo-e-u-king.

The Medicine or "Healing" comparison.

Delivered at Sravasti. Translated as before. pp. 2.

(d) Fo-shwo-kun-teng-wang-king.

The comparison of the Anointed King (or Baptized) [Abhisheka.]

Delivered at Sravasti. Translated as before. p. 1.

(e) Fo-shwo-ni-kiu-to-Fan-chi-king.

Buddha recites the Nirgrantha Brahmachari Sûtra (or, it may be, the Sûtra of t Brahmachari Nyagrodha.)

Delivered in the Kalandavenuvana, near Râjagriha. Translated by Shi-hu, of the Su dynasty. In 2 Parts; pp. 16.

(f) Fo-shwo-pih-i-kin-chwong-i-po-lo-man-un-hi-king.

Buddha recites the history of the two Brahmans Pih-i (white-clad), and Kin-chwo (golden standard).

Translated as before. In 2 Parts; pp. 21.

(g) Fo-shwo-fuh-lih-t'ai-tseu-yin-un-king.

Buddha recites the History of the Kumâra Fuh-lih (strength of bliss.)

Translated as before. In 3 Parts; pp. 23.

(h) Fo-shwo-shin-mao-hi-kin-king.

Buddha repeats the Sûtra called "That which makes the Hair of the Body stand ere for joy."

Delivered in the "very excellent" grove of the great city of the country of Vaisa Translated by Wei-tsing and others, of the Sung dynasty. Parts 3; pp. 31.

2. Pah-king.

Eight Sûtras, of which the following are most important:—

(a) Fo-shwo-kwong-ming-tchung-tseu-yin-un.

Buddha relates the History of the Youth, Young Man, Kwong Ming (Prabhâsa (?).)

Delivered in the Kalandavenuvana, near Râjagriha. Translated by Shi-hu, of the Sur dynasty. In 4 Chapters (Kiouen); pp. 40.

(b) Fo-shwo-tso-fun-shwo-king.

This is the History of the Kasyapas and their conversion, with the subsequent events in Buddha's career down to the conversion of Mogalan and Sariputra. In 2 Parts; pp. 19

3. Kiu-king.

Nine Sûtras (principally Dharanis.)

4. (a) Fo-shwo-tai-tsah-ui-tching-fa-king.

Buddha declares the great accumulated assembly (of) the True Law.

Translated by Shi-hu, of the Sung dynasty. In five Caps.; pp. 56.

(b) Khe-i-kwan-tseu-tsai-pu-sah-king.

Certain dharanis delivered by Avalokiteshwara, and called "*Khe-i.*"

Translated by Puh-hung, of the Tang dynasty. pp. 10.

(c) Pi-sha-man-tien-wang-king.

The Sûtra of the Devaraja Vaisravana, or Visvakarman.

Translated as before. pp. 6. [The above consists of Dhâranis, or 'true words, delivered by Vaisravana.]

(d) Man-ju-man-king-tsze-moo-p'hin.

The questions of Manjusri relating to the Mother-letters which enter into all sounds.

[These, in fact, are the letters of the Sanscrit alphabet.] Translated as before. pp. 3.

5. Hai-i-pu-sa-sho-wen-king.

Aryasagaramati paripritchch'a Sûtra.

Translated by Fa-hu, of the Sung dynasty. 1 Volume; 5 Caps.

6. Fo-shwo-tchu-kai-chang-pu-sah-sho-wen-king.

Ratnamegha nama mahâyana Sûtra. (*Julien, Concordance* No. 161.)

Translated by various Priests of the Sung dynasty. 2 Volumes; 20 Caps.

7. Ta-shing-mi-yen-king.

Ghana vyûha nama mahâyana Sûtra.

Translated by Amoghavajra, of the Tang dynasty. 1 Volume; 3 Parts. pp. 25, 31, 30.

8. Shau-hu-kwo-kai-chu-to-lo-ni-king.

A work containing dhâranis.

Translated by Prajna and other Priests, of the Tang dynasty. 2 Volumes; 10 Caps.

9. Ta-shing-pen-sing-sin-ti-kwan-king.

A work on Samadhi.

Translated by Prajna and others, of the Tang dynasty. 2 Volumes; 8 Kiouen.

10. Jin-wang-hou-kwo-pan-jo-king.

A Sûtra of the Prajna paramita class, to be used by a monarch for the protectioı of his country.

Translated by Amoghavajra, of the Tang dynasty. 1 Volume; 3 Parts. pp. 17 anc 21 (apparently only 2 Parts.)

11. Ti-tsong-pu-sa-pen-un-king.

The personal vows of Ti-tsong Bôdhisatwa (Chitigarbha (?).)

1 Volume; 2 Parts. Translated by Sikshananda, of the Tang dynasty. pp. 23 and 20

12. Hai-i-pu-sa-sho-wen-king.

Sagaramati, &c. (same as 5.)

13. Pah-king.

Eight Sûtras, principally containing dhârani. 1 Volume.

14. Shi-wu-king

Fifteen Sûtras, in 1 Volume. The principal ones are these:—

(a) Fo-shwo-sheng-kiun-wang-sho-wen-king.

The questions of Prasenajita.

(b) Fo-shwo-lun-wang-tsi-pao-king.

The seven treasures of a Chakravartin.

(c) Fo-shwo-un-sing-shu-king.

Concerning the Tree that grows in the Trayastrinshas Heaven, called *Yuen-sing*, [garden-birth.]

(d) Fo-shwo-ta-kin-ku-Po-lo-men-un-hi-king.

The History of the Brahman called Ta-kin-ku (Mahadruva (?).)

All these were translated during the Sung dynasty. 1 Volume; pp. 85.

15. Five short Sutras on magic (Tantra.)

XXXVIII.

Ta-shing-li-tseu-luh-po-lo-mi-to-king.

A work of the Mahayana School, or the six paramitas. 3 Volumes; 10 Kiouen.

Yih-tsai-ju-lai-tai-kiau-wang-king.

The teaching of all the Buddhas. 5 Volumes; 30 Kiouen.

Pu-sah-tsong-ching-fa-king.

Bôdhisatwa pitaka mahayana Sûtra (?). In 6 Volumes; 40 Kiouen.

Yih-tsai-ju-lai-ta-man-to-lo-king.

Sarvatathâgata mahamandala Sûtra.

1 Volume. Translated during the Sung dynasty.

(*a*) **Fo-shwo-tai-shing-shi-yin-king.**

Mahâyana prajnamudra Sûtra. (?)

(*b*) **Fa-shing-i-kue-teng-king.**

(*c*) **Ta-pih-san-koi-tsung-chi-to-lo-ni.**

The great White Umbrella Dharani.

The above (*a*), (*b*), (*c*), are in 1 Volume.

(*a*) **Ta-shing-tsui-chun-sun-shwo-chu-fa-king.**

(*b*) **Ta-shing-jih-chu-Fo-keng-kai-chi-kwong-ming-king.**

The above, in 1 Volume, belong to the Mahayana System, but are of no importance.

XXXIX.

1. Ta-p'ao-kwang-po-pi-mi-to-lo-ni-king.

Mahâ mani vipulya vimâna visva supratishthita guhyam paramarahasyam kalpa râja nama dhârani *(Concordance* 641.*)*

There is a curious plate on the first page of this work, which illustrates the Thibetan Formula "Om mani padme houm." Translated by Puh-hung (Amogha), of the Tang dynasty. 1 Volume; 3 Parts.

2. Yih-tseu-ki-te-fo-ting-king.

Ushnishachakravarttitantra. *(Concordance* 222.*)*

1 Volume; 3 Parts. Translated by Puh-hung, of the Tang dynasty.

3. Yu-kia-ta-kiau-wang-king.

A work on Yoga, and name by *Julien (Concordance* 878*)*, "Mayadjala mahâ tantra mah yana gambhira naya gouhya paraçi nama *m.y.s.*"

1 Volume; 5 Chapters. Translated by Fa-hu, of the Sung dynasty.

4. Po-ti-ch'ang-sho-shwo-yih-tseu-ting-lun-wang-king.

Probably the same as No. 2, above. 1 Volume; 5 Chapters. Translated by Puh-hun of the Tang dynasty.

5. Miau-kie-tsiang-ta-kiau-wang-king.

The same as 357 in *Julien's Concordance.* 1 Volume; 3 Chapters. Translated l Sse-kien, of the Sung dynasty.

6. Kin-kang-san-nieh-pi-mih-ta-kiau-wang-king.

Probably the same as *Concordance* 284, viz., "Bhuta damara tantra *n.m.y.* Sûtra 2 Volumes; 7 Chapters. Translated by Shi-hu, of the Sung dynasty.

[There are 10 other Volumes in this case, all of the same character as the abov belonging to the Tantra system.]

XL.

Fo-shwo-ju-lai-puh-sz'-i-pi-mih-ta-shing-king.

Buddha recites the Sûtra of the great Vehicle (Mahayana) called "The great an incomprehensible mysteries of (the person and Mission) of Tathagata."

This work, which is in two Books, 20 Chapters (Kiouen), and 25 Sections, contains a account of the various excellences of Buddha's person, mode of teaching, languag preaching, &c., with details respecting Ajatasatrurâja and others.

It was translated by Fa-hu and others, of the Sung dynasty.

Ta-fang-kwong-man-chu-i-kwai-king.

Traces of the secret (esoteric) teaching of Manjusri, a Sûtra of the Vaipulya class.

This work is in 3 Books and 20 Chapters (Kiouen.) It was translated by Sih-tsai, the Sung dynasty.

Fo-shwo-Tsun-na-pu-sah-i-kwai-king.

Buddha recites the Sûtra known as the secret (esoteric) doctrine of the Bodhisatwa Tsun-n

Originally composed by Nagarjuna, and translated by Fa-kien, of the Sung dynast In 4 Chapters; 1 Volume.

Pin-na-ye-kia-tien-i-kwai-king.

The Sutra containing the secret or Esoteric teaching of the Deva Pinnayaka.

Translated by Fa-kien, of the Sung dynasty. In 4 Chapters (Kiouen); 1 Volume.

Kin-kong-hiang-pu-sah-i-kwai-king.

Traces of the Esoteric teaching of the Bodhisatwa Kin-kong-hiang (Vajraghanda (?).)

Translated as before. 3 Parts; 1 Volume.

Ta-shing-yu-kia-kin-kong-sing-hai-ta-kiau-wong-king.

A work on Yoga. Translated by Puh-hung (Amogha), a Priest of the Tang dynasty. In 10 Chapters; 2 Volumes.

(*a*) **Ta-pi-hung-chi-i-kwai-king.**

(*b*) **Fan-no-ming-wang-i-kwai-king.**

Two Sûtras, in 1 Volume, on Yoga. Translated by Fa-hu, of the Sung dynasty.

(*a*) **Man-chu-shi-li-king.**

(*b*) **Yih-tsai-fuh-shih-siang-ying-king.**

(*c*) **Shi-tsz'-mu-king.**

(*d*) **'An-siang-san-mui-i kwai.**

(*e*) **Kin-chi-niu-wang-king.**

(*f*) **Shi-yih-mien-kwan-tsz'-tsai-mih-in.**

(*g*) **Nien-tung-i-kwai.**

Seven Sûtras, in 1 Volume, principally on Yoga, and containing dhârani. The Sûtra, marked (*c*), is curious as giving the old form of Sanscrit Letters, with the sounds and the virtues of these letters (in magic) attached. Translated by Puh-hung (Amogha), of the Tang dynasty.

Shi-tsah-king.

Seventeen Sûtras, containing Dharanis, principally laudatory stanzas in honor of Avalokiteshwara. There is one of these called "Pah-ta-ling-tah-fan-tsan." *i.e.*, "Sanscrit laudatory verses in honor of the eight sacred places (chaityas"), composed by *Siladitya Raja*, translated by Fa-kien, of the Sung dynasty. These verses are transliterated into Chinese, and may be restored to their original Sanscrit.

(*a*) **Shing-pao-shin-i-kwai-king.**

(*b*) **Pao-tsong-shin-man-no-lo-i-kwai-king.**

(*c*) **Kin-kong-hung-po-tsui-shing-sin-ming-wong-king.**

Three Sûtras, in one Volume, containing dhâranis and magical words. Translated by Fa-tien, of the Sung dynasty.

(*a*) **Ta-wai-lih-niu-chu-shih-ma-ming-wang-king.**

(*b*) **Kwan-siang-man-na-lo-tsing-tchu-ngok-tsu-king.**

Two Sûtras, in one Volume, containing dhâranis and magic sentences. The first translated by A-chi-tah-sien (Ajitatsin (?)), of North India (no date.) The second by Fa-kien, of the Sung dynasty.

(a) **Pu-sah-niu-kiai-king.**

(b) **Yau-po-sah-wu-kiai-wai-i-king.**

(c) **Man-chu-tsing-liu-king.**

Three Sûtras, in 1 Volume, containing Rules of conduct for a Bôdhisatwa and Upasaka: (a) and (b) translated by Gunavarma (?) of Gandhara, in the Sung dynasty the third (c), translated by Fa-hu (Dharmaraksha), of the Western Tsin dynasty, 220 A.D

(a) **Miau-kih-tsang-yu-kia-ta-kiau-kin-king.**

(b) **Tai-li-san-mui-na-wai-no-wang-shi-tche.**

(c) **Shing-kia-ni-fan-kin-kong-chung-tseu.**

Three Sûtras, in 1 Volume, containing dhârani, and generally on Yoga. Translated b Fa-tien, of the Sung dynasty.

XLI.

Fo-ts'ang-king.

Buddha pitakanaigraha *n.m.* Sûtra.

A work of the Vinaya class. Translated by Kumârajiva. 1 Volume; 4 Kiouen.

Yau-po-sah-kiai-king.

Rules for the Upasikawas.

Translated by Dharmaraksha, of the Northern Leung dynasty. 2 Volumes; 8 Kiouen

Shi-song-liu.

Sarvâstivâdavinaya.

A copy of the Rules of the Vinaya known as the "Ten Recitations." Translated b Kumârajiva. 5 Volumes; 20 Kiouen.

Pu-sah-ti-chi-king.

A work of the Vinaya class, called 'Bôdhisatvâcharyya nirdesa.' Translated b Dharmaraksha. 4 Volumes; 8 Kiouen.

Fan-kong-king.

The Brahmajâla Sûtra (although classified with the Vinaya works.)

Translated by Kumârajiva. 1 Volume; 2 Parts.

Pu-sah-sheu-kiai-king.

This is said, by *Stas. Julien (Concordance* 476, 487, 486*)*, to be the same as that give above, "Bôdhisatvâcharyya nirdesa. 3 Volumes; 10 Kiouen.

Luh-king-tung-pen.

Six Sûtras, the same original (*i.e.*, the same cover or leaves)—

1. The questions of Upali.
2. The Rules of the Sarvastivadina School.
3. The Rules of the Kasyâpiyas.
4. Transgressions of the Law (Dharma), light and serious.
5. Kiai-siu-tsae-king *i.e.*, Evils accruing on transgressions of the Law.
6. The five Rules of the Upisakawa.

[All the above belong to the Vinaya, and are of importance]

Pah-king-tung-pen.

Eight short Sutras (Vinaya.)

[Four Volumes, containing Sûtras, principally relating to the conduct of Bôdhisatw (Numbered on the covers, O., P., Q., R.)]

XLII.

Shi-song-liu.

Sarvastivadavinaya.

Translated by Kumarajiva. 13 Volumes; 65 Kiouen.

Ni-kie-mo.

Rules for the Bikshunis.

1 Volume; 5 Kiouen. Translated by various Shamans of the Tang dynasty.

XLIII.

Mo-ho seng-chi-liu.

The Vinaya, according to the School of the Mahasanghikas.

Translated partly by Fa-hien, and partly by Buddhabhadra, of the Eastern Tsin dyna: 15 Volumes; 40 Kiouen. [Deserves analysis.]

XLIV.

Sse-fen-liu-tsong.

The Vinaya Pitaka, according to the School of the Dharmaguptas.

Translated by Buddhayasa, together with Chu-Fo-nien (Buddhasmitti (?)), of the pe Tsin-yaou (*circ.* 410 A.D.) 15 Volumes; 30 Kiouen.

XLV.

Kan-ken-pi-nai-ye-tsa-sse.

Selections from the Vinayapitaka, as known in the Mûlasarvastivadina School.

12 Volumes; 40 Kiouen. Translated by I-tsing, of the Tang dynasty.

Ni-sha-sah-po-wu-fen-liu.

The Vinaya, according to the Mahisasika School. 9 Volumes; 30 Kiouen.

Translated by Buddhajiva and another, of the Sung dynasty.

XLVI.

Kan-pen-shwo-yih-tsai-yeou-po-pi-ni-ye.

The Vinaya Pitaka, according to the School of the Mûlasarvastivadins.

15 Volumes; 50 Kiouen. Translated by I-tsing, of the Tang dynasty.

Sz'-fen-liu-tsong.

The Vinaya Pitaka, known as the "Four divisions" [*i.e.*, of the Dharmagupta School.]

Translated during the period Yaou-tsin (405 A.D.), by the Shamans Buddhayasa and Chu-Fo-nien. 3 Volumes only; from 51 to 60 Kiouen.

XLVII.

Kan-pen-sa-po-ta-po-liu-shi.

Sarvastivadavinaya samgraha.

Translated by I-tsing, of the Tang dynasty. 4 Books; 14 Kiouen. Composed by Jinamitra.

Kan-pen-shwo-yih-tsai-yeou-po-pi-kiu-ni-pei-ni-ye.

Mûlasarvâstivâdabhikshunivinaya.

Translated by I-tsing, of the Tang dynasty. 6 Volumes; 20 Kiouen.

Shen-kin-pi-po-sha-liu.

Vibâshavinaya.

Translated by Sanghabhadra. In 7 Books; 18 Kiouen.

Kan-pen-shwo-yih-tsai-yeou-po-pi-nai-ye-po-sang-sse.

Sanghapitakasvastu [*Julien, Concordance* 261.] This work refers to various *trangressions* of the Law, by Priests and others. 6 Books; 20 Kiouen. Translated by I-tsing, of the Tang dynasty.

Sse-fen-sang-kie-mo.

Dharmaguptabhikshu karmma (*Concordance* 548.)

Translated by certain Shamans, of the Tang dynasty. 2 Books; 5 Kiouen.

Kiai-in-un-king.

Vinayanidâna Sûtra [according to *Julien*, *Concordance* 276. But the work is actually an account of the various events or occurrences which led to the different Rules in the Pratimoksha. Some of these events are given by Gogerley, at the end of his translation of the Pratimoksha.]

Translated by Chu-Fo-nien, of the Yaou-tsin period, *circ.* 404. 3 Books; 10 Kiouen.

Sse-fen-pi-kiu-ni-ki-mo-fa.

Dharmagupta bhikshuni karmma.

Rules for the Bhikshunis, according to the Dharmagupta School. 1 Book; 1 Kiouen.

Ta-pi-kiu-san-tsin-wei-i.

3,000 Rules for the guidance of the Great Bhikshus. (?)

Translated by 'Ngan-shai-ko, of the after Han dynasty. (The Sangha School (Mahasangha (?)), say that the translator's name is lost. 1 Volume; 1 Kiouen.

XLVIII.

Sah-po-to-pi-ni-pi-po-sha.

The "Vinayavibasha," according to the school of the Sarvastivadins.

3 Volumes; 8 Kiouen. The translator's name lost.

Sah-po-to-po-pi-ni-ma-teh-lai-kia.

The Vinaya Matrika, according to the School of the Sarvastivadins.

Translated by Sanghavarmma, of the Tang dynasty. 3 Volumes; 10 Kiouen.

Kan-pen-yeou-po-mu-teh-kia.

The Vinaya Matrika, according to the Mûlasarvastivadin School.

Translated by I-tsing, of the Tang dynasty. 1 Volume; 5 Kiouen.

Kan-pen-yeou-po-ni-to-na.

The Nidânas, according to the Mûlasarvastivadins.

Translated as before. 1 Volume; 5 Kiouen.

Kan-pen-yeou-po-pi-ni-ye-song.

Chants or verses respecting the Vinaya as used by the Mûlasarvastivadins.

Originally composed by the honorable Vaisaka. Translated by I-tsing, of the Tang dynasty. 2 Volumes; 4 Kiouen.

Kan-pen-pih-yih-kie-ma.

101 Rules as used by the Mulasarvastivadins.

2 Volumes; 7 Kiouen. Translated by I-tsing, of the Tang dynasty.

Pi-ni-mu-lun.

Vinaya Matrika Shastra.

Translator's name lost. 2 Volumes; 8 Kiouen.

Sha-mi-shi-kiai-fa-ping-wai-i-kie-ma.

10 Rules for the direction of the Samanera, and also regulations for his decorous behaviour.

Translator's name lost. The Title, however, appears in the Eastern Tsin dynasty 1 Volume; 2 Parts.

(1) Suh-sah-po-to-pi-nie.

A continuation of the Rules of the Vinaya, as accepted by the Sarvastivadins.

(2) Kan-pen-pi-kiu-tsa-hio-leuh-fa.

Brief Rules for the Bhikshu, in practising wisdom (Bôdhi), according to the Mula sarvastivadins.

The two preceding in one volume. No author's name given. [Deserve further attention]

(a) **Tan-wou-teh-liu-po-ts'a-kie-mo.**

Various Rules of the Dharmagupta School—from the Vinaya.

(b) **Sha-mi-wai-i.**

Rules for the behaviour of the Samanera.

(c) **Sha-ma-ni-tsi-kiai-man.**

Various Rules for the female disciple.

(d) **Shi-song-kie-ma-pi-kiu-iu-yung.**

Rules for the admission of the Bhikshu (*i.e.*, his ordination.)

The above, in 1 Volume. Translated during the Wei and Sung dynasties.

(a) **Liu-i-shi-i-ming-liu-lun.**

Twenty-two discourses on the Vinaya.

(b) **Kan-pen-po-ni-to-na-shi-song.**

Some verses on the Nidanas, according to the Mûlasarvastivadins.

(c) **Kan-pen-po-pi-ni-ye-shi-song.**

Some verses on the Vinaya of the Mûlasarvastivadins.

(d) **P'o-kien-pu-sah-hing-un-tsan.**

Some verses in praise of Samantabhadra Bôdhisatwa.

The above are in one Volume. Translated during the Tsin and Tang dynasties.

(a) **Shi-song-liu-pi-kiu-kiai-pen.**

Rules for the Bhikshus (Pratimoksha), according to the Mahasanghikas (so it appears 'Shi-song' is to be rendered: compare the first and second translations in this Book.)

(b) **Similar Rules for the Bhikshuni.**

(c) **Ta-sha-men-pih-yih-kie-ma-fa.**

Rules for the Great Shamans.

The above, in one Volume. Translated during the Eastern Tsin and Tang dynasties.

(a) **Kan-pen-shwo-yih-tsai-yeou-po-pi-kieu-ni-kiai-king.**

Rules for the Bhikshunis, according to the Mûlasarvastivadins.

(b) **Rules for the Bhikshunis, according to the Mahasanghikas.**

(c) **Sha-mi-ni-kiai-king.**

Rules for the Female Novice.

[I do not find the second of these works in the Book, although the Title stands on the cover. S.B.]

The above, in one Volume. Translated during the Tang and Eastern Tsin dynasties.

(a) **Fo-shwo-ta-'ai-tao-pi-kiu-ni-king.**

The Sûtra of the Mahaprajapati Bhikshuni.

(b) **Mu-kin-man-kiai-liu-chung-wu-pih-hing-chung-sse-king.**

Five hundred questions by Mogalan.

The above, in one Volume. The Translator's name lost.

(*a*) **Sz'-fen-kiai-pen.**

This is the Pratismoksha (according to the School of the Dharmaguptas, *Julien.*)

(*b*) **Rules for the Bhikshunis.**

These two, in one Volume.

(*a*) **She-li-fuh-man-king.**

The questions of Sariputra.

(*b*) **Mi-sha-sa-kie-ma-pen.**

Rules of the Mahisasika School.

The above, in one Volume. The latter translated during the Tang dynasty. It would appear that the Mahisasikas are also called the School of the *five* divisions, in distinction to the School of *four* divisions. This last work deserves attention, as it seems to agree still closer with the Southern version of the Pratimoksha.

(*a*) **'Ng-fen-kiai-pon.**

Rules according to the School of the five divisions, *i.e.*, the Mahisasikas.

(*b*) **Rules for the Bhikshunis.**

(*c*) **Pi-lo-ti-muh-c'ha-sang-ki-kiai-pen.**

The Pratimoksha, according to the Mahâsanghikas. [But the work itself is called "Sz-fen-pi-kiu-ni-kiai-pen." There seems to be a mistake in the binding up of this Volume, as the above is the *second* part, and no first part is given].

The above are in 1 Volume. The second translated during the Sung dynasty. Translator's name erased.

XLIX.

Tai-chi-to-lun.

The Mahâprajnaparamita Shastra.

This work, which was composed by Nagarjuna Bôdisatwa, and translated into Chinese by Kumârajiva, appears to be an exegesis of the Prajnaparamita Sûtra. (It deserves attention.) 15 Volumes; from Kiouen 1 to Kiouen 44.

Kin-kong-i-lun.

Two Shasters on the Vajrachhedika Sûtra.

The first by Asangha. The second by Vasubandhu. The first translated by Dharmajita, of the Tsui dynasty; the second by Bôdhirutchi, of the Wei period. [Observe, this Volume appears to be out of its place in this cover, as the number of Volumes is complete (according to the Table of Contents) without it. S.B.]

L.

Yu-kia-ssi-ti-lun.

The Yogâcharyya bhumi Shastra.

Composed by Maitreya Bôdhisatwa, and translated into Chinese by Hiouen Thsang, of the Tang dynasty. 20 Volumes ; 100 Kiouen.

LI.

Ta-chi-to-lun.

Mahâjnanaprasthana Shastra.

Composed by Nagarjuna, and translated by Kumârajiva, of the Yaou-Tsin period. 19 Volumes ; 100 Kiouen.

LII.

Shi-ta-shing-lun-shih.

Mahâyana samparigraha Sastra. (?)

This work seems to be partly composed by Asangha Bodhisatwa, and partly by his brother, Vasubandhu. *Julien*, I., p. 115, speaks of it as the work of Vasubandhu. *Eitel*, Handbook (68 *b*), says it is ascribed to Asangha. But there is an introduction in Kiouen 11, which seems to indicate that the original work was revealed by Maitreya Bodhisatwa to Asangha, and that the present treatise, which is an expansion of the original, is by his brother, Vasubandhu.

14 Volumes ; 48 Kiouen. Translated, as it appears, partly by Hiouen Thsang, and partly by Chin-ti, of the Tang dynasty and the Tsui dynasty, respectively.

Wu-lun.

Five short Shasters, of which the two last deserve examination, viz., the Ta-shing. kwang-wu-wen-lun, *i.e.*, Panchasknandha vaipulya Sastra ; and the Ta-shing-wu-wen-kingt *i.e.*, Mahayana panchaskandha Sastra.

The first was composed by Vasubandhu Bodhisatwa, and translated by Hiouen Thsang ; the second was composed by 'An-hwui (Sthitamati Bodhisatwa, *Julien*, I, 212), and translated by Devakara.

[We have in these two Shasters, excellent definitions of the elements of existence, or the phenomenal world.]

LIII.

Shi-chu-pi-po-sha-lun.

Dasabhumi vibasha Shastra.

Composed by Nagarjuna, and translated into Chinese by Kumârajiva. 4 Volumes ; 15 Kiouen.

Po-tai-tsz'-liang-lun.

A discourse on the peculiar properties of Bôdhi.

Composed by Nagarjuna, but arranged in its present order by the Bhikshu, Isvara Translated by Dharmagupta, of the Tsui dynasty, 580 A.D. 2 Volumes; 6 Kiouen.

Hien-yang-ching-kiau-lun.

A Shastra written by Asangha, and translated by Hiouen Thsang (*Vid. Julien*, I., 11ℓ 122, 164.) 4 Volumes; 20 Kiouen.

Chong-lun.

Pranyamûlasâstratikâ.

Composed by Nagarjuna. Translated by Kumârajiva. 2 Volumes; 4 Kiouen.

Ta-shing-o-pi-ta-mo-ts'a-tsi-lun.

Mahâyanabhidharma sangitiS astra.

Composed by a Bôdhisatwa called Gan-hwui, and translated by Hiouen Thsang 5 Volumes; 16 Kiouen.

LIV.

Ta-shing-chwong-yan-king-lun.

Mahâyana alamkara Sûtra Shastra.

A discourse on the Alamkara Sûtra by the Bôdhisatwa Asangha. Translated b Prabhâkalamitra, of the Tang dynasty. It is in 5 Volumes, and 13 Kiouen. [Sutralam kâra tika] *Julien.*

Ta-chwong-yen-king-lun.

Mahâlamkara Sûtra Shastra.

By Asvagosha Bôdhisatwa. Translated by Kumârajiva, 404 A.D. (Sutralamkar Shastra) *Julien.* In 4 Volumes; 13 Kiouen.

Pan-jo-tang-lun.

Prajnadipa Shastra.

By Nagarjuna. Translated by Prabhakalamitra, of the Tang dynasty. In 5 Volumes 15 Kiouen.

[Prajnapradipaçastrakarika of *Julien*, (peut etre).]

(*a*) Shi-'urh-men-lun.

A discourse on twelve methods of religious instruction, or (according to *Julien*, 6(San. Sin. dict.), dissertation on the twelve philosophical Schools [Dvadaçanikâyaçastra *Julien.*]

Written by Nagarjuna. Translated by Kumârajiva. 1 Chapter; pp. 32.

(b) Shi-pah-hung-lun.

A discourse on the eighteen kinds of 'void.' [Achtadaçâkâcasastra, *Julien.*]

Translated by Chin-ti, of the Chin dynasty. 1 Chapter; pp. 22.

(a) Man-chu-sse-li-man-po-ti-king-lun.

A discourse on the Sûtra which relates to the questions of Manjusri concerning Bodhi. [Manjusri paripritchch'a Sûtra Sastra (?)]

In two Parts; pp. 19, and pp. 16. Composed by Vasubandhu, and translated by Bodhirutchi, of the Wei dynasty, *circ.* 200 A.D.

(b) Kin-kong-po-ye-po-tsu-cho-lun.

A work written by Kung-tih-shi Bodhisatwa, and translated by a Shaman called Devakara, of Mid. India. In two Parts; pp. 20 and 19.

She-ta-shing-lun.

Mahâyana samparigraha Sastra.

In three Parts; 2 Volumes; pp. 23, pp. 18, pp. 25. Translated by Chin-ti, of the Chin dynasty.

Shing-sse-wei-fan-tien-so-wen-king-lun.

According to *Julien*, this ought to be restored to Arya visechachinti Brahmana paripritchch'a Sûtra tika. Literally, it is a discourse on the Sûtra relating to the questions of the excellently wise Brahma Deva.

Translated by Bodhirutchi, of the Wei dynasty. In 3 Parts; 1 Volume; pp. 24, 23, 22.

(a) Pe-lun.

Satashastra. (?)

A hundred discourses by Deva Bodhisatwa. Translated by Kumârajiva. In two Parts; pp. 29 and 23.

(b) Kwang-pe-lun.

Another copy of the above, belonging to the Vaipulya class of works, restored by *Julien (peut etre)* to "Cataçastra Vaipulyam."

Composed by Deva Bôdhisatwas, and translated by Hiouen Thsang. 1 Chapter; pp. 15.

LV.

Kwang-pe-lun-shi-lun.

The Satasâstra vaipulyam, with a commentary.

This work was composed by Deva Bôdhisatwa, and the commentary by Dharmatrata.

Translated into Chinese by Hiouen Thsang. 3 Volumes; 10 Kiouen.

[This work deserves attention, as it is plainly written, and its method appears good.]

Shi-ti-king-lun.

Dasabhumaka Shaster.

Composed by Vasubandhu, and translated by Bôdhirutchi, of the Wei period. 4 Volumes; 12 Kiouen.

Fo-ti-king-lun.

Buddhabhumi Sûtra Sastra.

Composed by Prabhâmitra (so *Julien* renders *Thsin-kwang*, *Concordance* 170), and others. Translated into Chinese by Hiouen Thsang. 2 Volumes; 7 Kiouen.

Shing-wei-shi-lun.

Vidya matra siddhi Sastra. (?)

Composed by Dharmatrata and others. Translated into Chinese by Hiouen Thsang. 4 Volumes; 10 Kiouen.

Mi-lai-so-wan-king-lun.

Maitreya paripritchch'a Sûtra Sastra.

Translated by Bodhirutchi, of the First Wei period. 2 Volumes; 7 Kiouen.

O-pi-ta-mo-tsi-lun.

Abhidharma sangiti Sastra. (?)

Composed by Asangha Bodhisatwa, and translated by Hiouen Thsang. 2 Volumes; 8 Kiouen.

Luh-lun.

Six Shasters, viz.—

1. Wou-liang-sheu-king-yeou-po-ti-she.

Amitabhâ Sûtra Upadesa Shaster.

Composed by Vasubandhu, and translated by Bôdhirutchi.

2. Chun-fa-lun-king-yeou-pi-ti-she.

Dharmachakra pravartana Sûtra Upadesa.

Composed by Vasubandhu, and translated by Pi-mu-chi-sien and others, of the former Wei period.

3. Tai-pan-ni-pan-king-lun.

Mahaparinirvâna Sûtra Sastra.

Composed by Vasubandhu, and translated by Dharmabodhi, of the former Wei period.

4. Ni-pan-king-pen-yeou-kin-wou-kie-lun.

Another work on the Nirvana (as before.)

5. Neng-tun-kin-kong-pan-jo-po-lo-mi-to-king-lun-song.

Verses composed by Asangha Bôdhisatwa, on the Prajnaparamita vajracheddika Sûtra.

Translated by I-tsing, of the Tang dynasty.

6. Hien-kiau-king-lun.

A discourse on the Sûtra called the dying instructions of Buddha.

By Vasubandhu. Translated by Chin-ti, of the Tsui dynasty.

[Two other works, containing smaller discourses.]

LVI.

K'ieou-king-yih-shing-p'ao-sing-lun.

(According to *Julien*, *Concordance* 281.) Mahâyana uttara tantra Sastra.

Translated by Lih-na-ma-ti, of the early Wei period. 1 Volume; 5 Kiouen.

[The 5th Kiouen is in the next No. in Catalogue.]

Ta-shing-chang-chin-lun.

[This Volume begins with the 5th Kiouen of the preceding work.]

This Title I am unable to restore. The work was translated by Hiouen Thsang. 2 Parts.

Ta-p'ao-tsi-king-lun.

Maharatnakûta Shastra. (?)

Translated by Bodhirutchi, of the former Wei period. 1 Volume; 4 Kiouen.

Shun-chung-lun.

Nyayaparyamulasastra. (?)

By Lung-shing, Nagajita (?), or Nagasena (?). Translated by Dharmaprajnarutchi, of the early Wei period. 1 Volume; 2 Parts.

Chung-pien-fen-pie-lun.

Madyânta vibhâga Shastra.

Composed by Vasubandhu Bôdhisatwa, and translated by Chun-ti, of the Tsui dynasty. 1 Volume; 2 Kiouen,

Fo-sing-lun.

Buddhaprakriti Shastra. (?)

1 Volume; 4 Kiouen. Composed by Vasubandhu Bodhisatwa. Translated Chun-ti, of the Tsui dynasty.

Shing-wei-shi-p'ao-sing-lun.

Vidyamatrasiddhi ratnajati Shastra. (?)

By Dharmapalita Bôdhisatwa. Translated by I-tsing, of the Tang dynas 1 Volume; 5 Kiouen.

Shih-ta-shing-lun-pen.

Mahâyâna samparigraha Sastra.

Composed by Asangha Bodhisatwa. Translated by Hiouen Thsang. 1 Volume; 3 Par

(*a*) See-ti-lun.

Chatursatya Sastra. (?)

Composed by Vasuvarmma, and translated by Chun-ti, of the Tsui dynasty.

(*b*) Pi-chi-Fo-in-youen-lun.

Pratyeka Buddha nidâna Sastra.

Composed and translated as in the preceding. [These two, in 1 Volume.]

(*a*) Pien-chung-pin-lun.

Madhyânta vibhâga Sastra. (?)

Composed by Vasubandhu, and translated by Hiouen Thsang.

(*b*) Pien-chung-pin-sung.

Madhyanta vibhâga grantha (*Julien* 454).

Composed by Vasubandhu Bôdhisatwa. [*Julien* says Maitreya Bôdhisatwa, *loc. cit* and translated by Hiouen Thsang.

LVII.

O-pi-ta-mo-ta-pi-po-sha-lun.

The Abhidharmamahâvibâsha Shastra.

Composed by the 500 Arhats at the first Council, and translated into Chinese l Hiouen Thsang, of the Tang dynasty. 20 Volumes; from Kiouen 1 to Kiouen 100.

LVIII.

O-pi-ta-mo-tai-pi-po-sha-lun.

The Abbidharmamahavibasha Shastra.

Composed by the 500 Rahats of the first Council, near Rajagriha, and translated by Hiouen Thsang, of the Tang dynasty. 20 Volumes; from Kiouen 100 to Kiouen 200.

LIX.

A-pi-tan-pi-po-sha-lun.

Abhidharma vibasha Shastra.

In 22 Volumes; 82 Kiouen. Composed by Katyâyanaputra; translated into Chinese by Buddhavarmma and another, of the Northern Liang dynasty. [This work is said to have been compiled at the time of the last Council, under Kanishka and Vasumitra (Hiouen Thsang, I., p. 26).]

LX.

Shun-ching-li-lun.

Nyâya anusâra Shastra.

A work by Sanghabhadra; translated by Hiouen Thsang, of the Tang dynasty. In 24 Volumes; 80 Kiouen.

LXI.

O-pi-ta-mo-tsong-hien-tsung-lun.

Abhidharma prakarana sasana Shastra.

By Sanghabadra; translated into Chinese by Hiouen Thsang. 12 Volumes; 40 Kiouen.

She-li-fo-a-pi-tan-lun.

Sariputrâbhidharma Shastra.

9 Volumes; 30 Kiouen. Translated by Dharmagupta and Dharmayasa.

O-pi-ta-mo-kiu-she-lun.

Abhidharmakosha Shastra.

Composed by Vasubandhu, and translated by Hiouen Thsang. 9 Books; 30 Kiouen.

LXII.

Shing-shih-lun.

Satyasiddha vyakarana Shastra.

A work of the Abhidharma class. In 7 Volumes; 20 Kiouen; 200 Sections. Composed by Aryavarma, and translated into Chinese by Kumârajiva.

'O-pi-t'an-mo-ku-she-shi-lun.

The Abhidharmakosha Shaster.

Composed by Vasubandhu; translated by Chin-ti, of the Tsui dynasty. In 7 Volume 22 Kiouen.

'O-pi-t'an-pah-kien-to-lun.

The Abhidharma jnana prasthâna.

Composed by Kâtyâyaniputra. In 8 Volumes; 30 Kiouen.

San-fa-to-lun.

Tridharmaka Sastra. (?)

Composed by "The Eminent *Parvatabhadra*" (?); translated by two Priests of t Eastern Tsin dynasty, called Sanghadeva, and Hwui-yuen. In 3 Parts; pp. 17, 18, 18.

San-mi-tai-po-lun.

Sammatiya Shastra.

A discourse on the School called Sammatiyas. In 3 Parts; pp. 12, 12, 1 Translator's name is lost.

LXIII.

1. Kan-lou-wei-lun.

Abhidharmâmrita Sastra.

Written by the Venerable Gosha, and translated by an unknown writer, during the W period. 1 Volume; 2 Parts.

2. A-pi-ta-mo-fa-chi-lun.

Abhidharma djnana prasthana.

Written by the Venerable Katyayaniputra; translated into Chinese by Hiouen Thsar of the Tang dynasty. 6 Volumes; 20 Kiouen.

3. Pi-po-sha-lun.

Vibashasastra.

Written by the Venerable Katyayaniputra, and translated into Chinese by Sanghabh danga, *circ.* 400 A.D. 5 Volumes; 14 Kiouen.

4. Tsa-i-men-tsuh-lun.

Abhidharma sangiti paryâya pada Sastra.

A work written by the Venerable Sariputra, and translated into Chinese by Hiou Thsang. 4 Volumes; 20 Kiouen.

5. Shi-shin-tsuh-lun.

Abhidharma vijnana kâya pada Sastra; or, according to the Catalogue, 'Tchi-yuen' Abhidharmamiti kâya pada.

Written by the Arhat Devasarman, and translated into Chinese by Hiouen Thsang 5 Volumes; 16 Kiouen.

6. Pin-lui-tsuh-lun.

Abhidharma prakaranapada Sastra.

Written by the Venerable Vasumitra, and translated into Chinese by Hiouen Thsang 5 Volumes; 18 Kiouen.

Tsui-siang-lun.

A work written by the Venerable Gunamiti, and translated into Chinese by Chin-ti, of the Tsui dynasty. 1 Volume; 2 Parts.

LXIV.

Tsun-po-siu-mi-so-tsi-lun.

Various Treatises by Aryavasumitra.

Translated by Sanghabhadanga, a Priest of Cabul (Kipin), in the Tsin dynasty 5 Volumes; 15 Kiouen.

Fa-ching-o-pi-tan-sin-lun.

Abhidharma hridaya Sastra.

Composed by the great Priest (Mahabhadanta) Upajita; translated by an Indian Priest called Nalandaryasa, during the dynasty or Rule of the Kao-tsai. 2 Volumes; 6 Kiouen

Tchong-sse-fen-o-pi-ta'n-lun.

Abhidharma prakarana pada.

Composed by Vasumitra; translated by two Priests of the Sung dynasty, viz. Gunabhadra and Bodhaya. 4 Volumes; 12 Kiouen.

Tsa-o-pi-ta'n-sin-lun.

Samyuktâbhidharma Sastra.

Composed by Arya Dharmatrata; translated by Sanghavarma and others, of the Sung dynasty. 5 Volumes; 11 Kiouen.

Lih-shi-o-pi-ta'n-lun.

A Treatise of the Abhidharma class, relating to the constitution of the Visible Kosmos Literally translated from the Chinese the title is "Establishing the world, Abhidharma Shastra."

It was translated by Chen-ti, of the Tsui dynasty. 3 Volumes; 10 Kiouen.

O-pi-t'an-sin-lun.

Abhidharmahridaya Sastra.

Composed by Fa-sheng, which, according to Julien *(Concordance)* pp. 383, is equal to Upajita; but it would seem to mean "Excellency of the Law," or "Victory of the Law" (?) Dharmajita.

Translated by Sanghadeva and another Priest, of the Eastern Tsin dynasty. 1 Volume 4 Kiouen.

Fen-pih-kung-te-lun.

A discourse respecting different grades of merit or excellency.

Translator's name lost. 1 Volume; 2 parts.

O-pi-t'an-mo-fa-wen-tsuh-lun.

Abhidharmaskandhapada.

Composed by Maudgalyana; translated by Hiouen Thsang. 3 Volumes: 10 Kiouen.

Jih-o-pi-t'an-ma-lun.

Abhidharmâvatara Sastra.

Composed by the Rahat Skandharata; translated by Hiouen Thsang. 1 Volume; pp. 16

Kiai-tuh-taou-lun.

Vimokshamarga Sastra. (?)

By the Rahat Upatissa; translated by Sangapala, of the Liang period. 3 Volumes 12 Kiouen.

Sheng-tsung-shi-ku-i-lun.

A treatise relating to the meaning of ten sentences belonging to the Abhidharma. (?)

By Djinaprajna chandra (?); translated by Hiouen Thsang. 1 Volume; pp. 13.

LXV.

Pou-sa-pen-sing-wan-lun.

Srimala Shastra. (?)

Composed by the Bodhisatwa Aryavarmma. 3 Volumes; 16 Kiouen.

Ta-shing-pa'o-in-i-lun.

A Shaster on the precious and desirable meaning of the Great Vehicle.

Translated during the Sung dynasty, by Fa-hu (Dharmagupta), and others. 1 Volume 10 Kiouen.

Iu-i-shi-lun.

A work on the Paramitas.

Originally composed by Naga Bodhisatwa, and translated into Chinese by 'Shi-hu,' the Sung dynasty. 1 Volume; 2 Parts.

Ta-shing-chung-kwan-shi-lun.

A treatise on the general doctrines of the Great Vehicle. Composed by a Bodhisatw called 'Gan-hwui (Rest-wisdom), and translated into Chinese by various Shamans of tl Sung dynasty. 1 Volume; 4 Parts.

Shi-sheh-lun.

A discourse on the virtue of Charity, or alms-giving; extracted from the "Abhidharn Shastra." [A very curious work, particularly the first Kiouen, which relates to tl Chakravartin, and appears to throw much light on the analogy between Tathâgata aı this Universal Monarch.]

Translated during the Sung dynasty. 1 Volume; 3 Parts.

Ta-shing-tsa-pou-sa-hwui-lun.

A discourse on various matters relating to the wisdom of Bôdhisatwa. 4 Volume 25 Kiouen.

Composed by Dharmayasa (?) Bôdhisatwa; translated during the Sung dynasty.

Ta-tsung-ti-un-man-pen-lun.

A discourse by Asvagosha Bôdhisatwa on esoteric doctrines of the Great Contemplati School (tsung (?).)

Translated by Chin-ti, of the Tsui dynasty. 1 Volume; 8 Kiouen.

Kin-tsa-shi-lun.

Literally, *Golden-seventy-shaster.*

It is a work by Kapila Rishi, and seems to contain an account of the Sankh Philosophy. 1 Volume; 3 parts. [Deserves attention.]

Kwang-shi-pu-sah-sin-lun.

A discourse on the Heart of Bodhi, by the Bôdhisatwa Padmasila, and translated the Sung dynasty, by Shi-hu. 4 Kiouen.

Pah-lun.

Eight discourses or Shasters, principally by Nâgârjuna Bôdhisatwa.

San-lun.

Three short discourses on Prajna, as the Mother of Buddha.

[Three other discourses on Yoga. The 3rd, named "Chang-sho-chi-lun," is a curio exposition of the origin of the world, and its present constitution.]

LXVI.

Fo-pen-hing-king.

This would seem to be a translation of the Buddhacharita, composed by Asvagosha. It is in seven Chapters, and translated into Chinese by Ratnamegha, a Shaman of Liang-cheu, of the Sung dynasty. 2 Volumes. [Deserves attention.]

The above work is composed in verse, and so translated. Burnouf states that the Buddhatcharita is composed in verses of the Anushtubh and Indravajra classes; in this translation this distinction is maintained throughout. 2 Volumes; 7 Chapters; 31 Sections.

Ch'uh-yau-king.

This signifies, literally, "The Dawn," or the "Birth of day." It is a copy of the Dhammapada, with the accompanying parables or avadânas. The Chinese Preface says that the first name given to this work was Ch'uh-yau, which is the same as Avadâna, the 6th of the 12 classes of Buddhist books. Afterwards it was put together in the shape of a work containing 1000 comparisons in 33 Sections, called *Fa-ku*, *i.e.*, Sections or Stanzas of the Law (Dhamma pada). It is said to have been composed by Dharmatrata Bodhisatwa, the uncle of Vasumitra. It was translated into Chinese by an Indian, of Ki-pin (Gandhara) called *Sanghabadanga* (?), otherwise, *Fo-nien* Buddhasmritti (?), who came to Lo-yang during the Yaou-Tsin period, *circ.* 400 A.D.

The work is in 7 Volumes; 20 Kiouen; and 33 Sections (p'in.)

Siu-hing-taou-ti-king.

Literally, "The Sutra which treats on the principles of Religious practice," It was composed, according to the prefatory remarks, by a Priest of Mid. India, called (by his personal name), Chung-hu, *i.e.*, Sanghapala, or (palita), of the city of Shing-hing (sacred prosperity (?) Sravasti). It was translated into Chinese by Fa-hu (Dharmaraksha), of the Western Tsin dynasty, *circ.* 220 A.D.

It is in 3 Volumes; 8 Kiouen; 30 Sections (p'in.)

Kien-yu-in-yun-king.

A copy of the work called Damamuka [Schmidt's "*der weise und der thor.*"]

In 4 Volumes; 13 Kiouen; 69 Sections. Translated into Chinese by Hwui-hioh, of the Wei dynasty. [It is a succession of tales of wise and foolish persons.]

Tsah-pao-tsong-king.

The Sutra called the "Treasury of miscellaneous jewels."

A collection of 121 tales or fables; translated into Chinese by two Shamans of the Wei dynasty.

These tales may have been translated elsewhere, but from a brief inspection of the Book, there are many I have never seen before. The last, *e.gr.*, is as follows:—

The Story of the slave girl fighting with the ram.

"Once upon a time, there was a certain slave girl, of a thrifty and careful disposition, who was employed by her master in storing the barley and the pulse. At the same time her Master kept a Ram, who was allowed to go at large, and who constantly came and eat the barley and the beans when the Maid was measuring them out. On this, the master was angry, because he did not believe that the waste was caused by the ram thus attacking the girl. Whereupon, the maid, being vexed, was in the habit of keeping a long stick by her side, with which she belaboured the beast whenever he came near her; and then, the ram getting savage, used to butt at and knock the girl about.

It happened, one day, when she was lighting a fire, and had no stick in her hand, that the ram, perceiving his opportunity, ran at the girl and butted her. On this, she took the fire-stick that was on the hearth and hit the creature over the head with it. Unluckily, this ignited the hair on his forehead, which made him run away through the house, and so he set the house on fire, and in this way the village was burnt down; and the fire, extending to a neighbouring wood, 500 monkeys, who lived in it, were surrounded by the flames and burnt to death. On seeing this sad sight, the Devas exclaimed, as follows :—

> " Anger leads to fighting,
> Which there is no stopping;
> The ram quarrelling with the girl,
> The men of the village and the monkeys are dead."

It is in 3 Volumes; 8 Chapters; 121 Sections.

Chan-tsah-pe-un-king.

The Sûtra which relates, in order, a collection of a hundred stories.

A hundred tales connected with the personal history of Buddha. [Some of them very amusing.]

In 2 Volumes; 10 Chapters; 100 Sections. Translated by Chi-hien, a Upasaka, of the Wu dynasty (the Getœ.)

(E) Shi-king-Tung-pen.

Ten short Sûtras; translated principally during the Tsin dynasty.

(D) Three short Sutras.

LXVII.

Wu-pan.

Five different brochures, belonging to the class 'cho-tsi' [*qu.* nipâta, or sannipâta.]

These essays or tracts belong to the tantra Period, and contain dhârani.

Shan-fa-iu-khai-king.

Important explanations of the laws or rules used by the Shan sect (contemplative School. *Edkins* identifies this School with the Jainas.) Translated by Kumârajiva. 1 Volume; 2 Parts.

Ta-mo-ta-lo-shan-king.

Given by *Julien (Concordance 636)*, as Dharmatâra dhyanasutra.

1 Book; 2 Parts. Translated by Buddhabhadra, of the Eastern Tsin dynasty.

Kin-kong-teng-tai-kiau-wang-king.

Rendered by *Julien (Concordance* 290), as 'Vajra sirsha mahâ guhya yoga tantra it might also be rendered 'Vajra ushnisha mahâguhya râja Sûtra.'

Translated by Amogha vajra, a Shaman of the Tang dynasty. 2 Parts.

Man-chu-sho-shwo-ngok-suh-yan-king.

A work on Astrology, by Manjusri. 1 Volume; 2 Parts

A-yu-wang-king.

Asokaraja Sûtra.

History of Asoka; translated by Sanghapâla. 2 Volumes; 10 Kiouen.

Sang-kia-lo-cha-Fo-hing-king.

A life of Buddha (Buddhatcharita), by Sangharaksha. [He lived 700 years after th Nirvana.]

Translated by Sanghabhadanga. 2 Volumes; 5 Kiouen.

Fo-sho-hing-tsan-king.

Buddhatcharita, by Asvagosha.

Translated by Dharmaraksha, or Dharmalatsin. 2 Books; 5 Kiouen.

Shiu-hing-pu-sah-hing-men-chu-king-iu-tsi.

Extracts from various Sûtras, respecting the probation of Bodhisatwa, ere h attained perfection. (Great Vehicle) 1 Volume.

Kiu-pan.

9 brief Sutras; principally of the Tautra Period.

Fa-keu-pi-hu-king.

The Parables attached to the verses of the Law, *i e.*, Dhammapadavâdana.

Translated by 2 Shamans of the Eastern Tsin dynasty, called Fa-khiu and Fa-lih 2 Volumes; 4 Kiouen.

Pou-ti-hing-king.

Bôdhicharita Sûtra. (?)

Translated during the Sung dynasty; Composed by Nâgarjuna Bodhisatwa. 1 Volume 4 Parts.

Fo-fa-tsong-yin-un-king.

An account of the transmission of the treasure of the Law, from generation to generation

[A work deserving attention.] 2 Volumes; 6 Kiouen. Translated during the earl Wei period, by two Shaman Priests, called *Kih-kia-ye*, and *Tan-yaou* (Dharmavadana (?)

Tso-shan-san-mui-fa-men-king.

Religious rules for practicing a samâdhi called "Tso-shan."

Composed by Sangharakshita; translated by Kumârajiva. 1 Volume; 2 Parts.

Na-sien-pi-khiu-king.

The Sûtra of the Bhikshu Na-sien.

The Translator's name is lost. 1 Volume; 3 Parts.

Seng-kia-sse-na-sho-chuen-pou-sa-pen-un-king.

Records of the Bôdhisatwas; compiled by Sanghasena. 1 Volume; 4 Kiouen.

(a) Pih-u-king.

Satâvadana Sutra.

A hundred stories; translated by Gunabhadra. (?) 2 Parts.

(b) Fa-keu-king.

Verses from the Law (Dharmapada.)

Composed by Dharmatrata, and translated by various Shamans of the Wu period 2 Parts.

Luh-king.

Six Sutras.

1. A-yu-wang-pi-u-king.

Asokavâdana Sûtra.

Translator's name lost.

2. San-hwui-king.

The Sûtra which discants on the 3 kinds of wisdom.

3. Wu-fa-hing-king.

Abhidharmapanchadharmatcharita Sûtra. (?)

Translated by Ngan-shi-ko, of the after Han dynasty.

4. Shwo-fa-un-king.

The history of Pindola (Bhara)dvadja, repeating the Law for the purpose of instructing the King Udayana.

Translated by Gunabhadra, of the Sung dynasty.

5. Tsung-pien-to-lu-king.

Questioning Pindola. Translated during the Sung dynasty.

6. Ta-yung-pu-sah-king.

The Sûtra of the Bôdhisatwa Ta-yung (in verse.)

Chung-king-chuen-tsa-pi-u-king.

Various stories selected from all the Sûtras. Translated by Kumarajiva.

A-yu-wang-wan-muh-yun-in.

Things which stirred Asokarâja to put out the eyes of his Son.

This is all in verse, 4 words to a line, and deserves notice.

A Volume, marked X., containing two treatises on Tantra, or later Buddhism.

T'sa-pi-u-king.

A miscellaneous collection of fables and stories.

The Translator's name is lost. It goes back, however, to the after Han dynasty.

Wou-ming-lo-cha-king.

Avidyaraksha Sûtra.

Wen-chu-sho-shwo-tsui-shing-ming-i-king.

Manjusrinamasangiti. Vid. *Julien (Concordance* 799.

Translated during the Sung dynasty.

Kiu-pan.

Nine Tracts, containing dhârani and charms.

Wu-king.

Five Sûtras.

1. Ku-ts'a-pi-u-king.

A book of ancient stories (miscellany.)

Translated by a Priest, Sang-ui, of the Wu period.

2. Shan-iu-ho-yuh-king.

3. Niu-shan-kwan-chang-keu-king.

4. Fa-kwan-king.

5. Kia-ye-kih-king.

[The above are of no great interest.]

Sze-A-Han-mo-liu-kiai.

Explanations of the four Agamas. 1 Volume; 2 Parts. Composed by Vasubandhu. (?

Kiu-pan.

Nine Treatises.

The first is on "The changes of the future; the second, "Miscellaneous stories;" the fourth, "Shi-'rh-yau" (12 journeys.) (?)

[These deserve attention.]

LXVIII.

1. Ti-tsong-pu-sah-pen-un-king.

An account of Kchittigarbha Bodhisatwa, and his conversations with the "Holy Mother' Mâya (Mother of Buddha), in the Trayastrinshas Heaven.

Translated by Sikshananda, of Khoten, during the Tang dynasty. 1 Volume.

2. Tsi-ku-kin-Fo-tan-lun-hung-shi-lu.

A history of the various Translators and eminent Buddhist Priests, who flourished in China, from the earliest period.

A Chinese work, written during the Tang dynasty. 2 Volumes; 4 Kiouen.

3. Sou-tsi-ku-kin-Fo-tau-lun-hung.

Continuation of the above. (Same period and author.) 1 Volume.

4. Ta-shing-pen-sing-sin-ti-kwan-king.

A work in 2 Volumes, and 8 Kiouen; translated by Prajna, of Gandhâra, and others, during the Tang dynasty.

(It is a work of the Mahâyana development, embracing metaphysical discussions with Maitreya and others.)

5. A-yu-wang-chun.

History of Asokarâja.

Translated by Ngan-fa-kin, of the Western Tsin dynasty, belonging to the Ngan-sih (Assika, Parthian) country. 2 Volumes; 5 Kiouen.

6. Yin-wang-hu-kwo-pan-jo-king.

A work of the Prajna paramita class; translated during the Tang dynasty. 1 Volume; 3 Parts.

7. Fo-ki-tsong-te-tsan.

Laudatory verses on Manjusri.

Composed by Tsih-yau (Munimitra (?)), and translated during the Sung dynasty. 1 Volume; 3 Parts.

8. Yen-k'au-shi-sih-i.

A work on the method of satisfying the wants of the Pretas (hungry ghosts, or creatures with flaming mouths); found in the Eastern Tsin Catalogue. Translator's name lost.

This work contains explanations of the charmed words and mudras used in Tantra Services. [The Sanscrit words are given in an archaic form.] 1 Volume.

9. Tsah-pan-tung-pen.

Seven essays, in 1 Volume.

The first is a memoir of Avagosha Bodhisatwa; the second, of Nagardjuna Bodhisatwa; the third, of Deva Bodhisatwa; the fourth, of Vasubandhu Bodhisatwa.

[The fifth and last essay in this Volume (although there are two additional Titles on the cover), is an address or lecture given by Nagardjuna to Jantakarâja (Shan-to-ka-wang.) This Title suggests the query whether Jantaka is another name for Melinda, in the *Melinda prasna* of the Southern School.] 1 Volume.

[The remaining eleven Volumes of this cover, containing 71 Sûtras, belong chiefly to the Yoga School, and contain mystical discussions.]

LXIX.

Chu-king-iu-ts'a.

Choice selections from all the Sûtras.

20 Volumes; 20 Kiouen. This interesting work contains a synopsis of the most important questions in Buddhism, and relies on passages selected from different Sûtras.

King-liu-i-siang.

Different extracts and comparisons drawn from the Sûtras and Vinaya.

A work in 15 Volumes; 50 Kiouen. It is a sort of epitome of the history of Buddhism, with an account of its persecutions in India. (Deserves separate analysis.)

To-lo-ni-tsi-ts'a.

A collection of Dharani. In 4 Volumes; 10 Kiouen.

LXX.

Chuh-san-tsong-ki-ts'a.

Various extracts and records connected with the Tripitaka.

Compiled by Sang-yau, of the Liang dynasty, 502 to 550 A.D. 5 Volumes; 17 Kiouen.

Puh-ying-pai-tsuh-tang-sse.

A work on Ritual. 2 Volumes; 6 Kiouen.

Kwang-sz-ming-ts'a.

The works of Sz'-ming, a Chinese Priest. 8 Volumes; 20 Kiouen.

(*a*) **Hien-mih-un-tung-shing-Fo-sin-iu-ts'a.**

A book on Tantra or Yoga.

(*b*) **Mih-chau-un-yin-wong-sing-ts'a.**

Another work on Yoga. The two, in 1 Volume. pp. 37 and 26.

Sz'-ming-ts'a.

Miscellaneous writings of Sz'-ming, a Chinese Priest. 5 Volumes; 14 Kiouen.

LXXI.

Kwang-sz-ming-ts'a.

Miscellaneous productions of Kwang-sze-ming. 8 Volumes; 40 Kiouen.

San-p'ao-han-tung-luh.

An account of different relics and sacred deposits found in different Temples (in China.) 2 Volumes; 4 Kiouen.

Ta-Tong-niu-tien-luh.

An Index of all Buddhist Books, translated into Chinese, up to the Tang dynasty. 5 Volumes; 16 Kiouen.

Khai-yuen-Shi-kiau-luh.

An Index of Buddhist Books, up to the Khai-yuen year of the Tang dynasty, 713-741 A.D.; translated into Chinese. 12 Volumes; 20 Kiouen.

LXXII.

Fa-yuen-chu-lin.

Pearls from the Garden of the Law.

18 Volumes; from Kiouen 1 to Kiouen 60, inclusive.

LXXIII.

Fa-yuen-chu-lin.

Pearls from the Garden of the Law (Dharma.)

A large Encyclopœdia, containing extracts from the entire Buddhist Canon.

This case contains 18 Volumes, viz., from Kiouen 61 to Kiouen 120, which is the end.

Compiled by various Shamans, of the Tang dynasty.

LXXIV.

Tsung-king-lu.

A connected history of the writings of the chief followers of the Tsung School, in China (*i.e.*, the Contemplative or Shan sect of Buddhists.) 8 Volumes; 30 Kiouen.

Ku-kin-shi-king-t'u-ki.

A catalogue of Buddhist Books (new and old.) Compiled by a Shaman of the Tang dynasty, called Tsing-mae. 2 Volumes; 4 Kiouen.

Suh-ku-kin-shi-king-t'u-ki.

A brief epitome of the above. 1 Kiouen.

Khai-yuen-shi-kiau-lu-lioh-chuh.

An epitome of the catalogue of Buddhist Books, known as the " Khai-yuen-lu. 2 Volumes; 4 Parts.

LXXV.

Tsung-keng-lu.

A connected history of the writings of eminent Priests of the Tsung School (Contemplative or ' Shan' (Jaina (?)) sect.) 21 Volumes; 100 Kiouen.

[This case contains only from Kiouen 31 to Kiouen 100, inclusive.]

LXXVI.

Kao-Seng-chou'en.

An account of the High Priests or Patriarchs, of the Buddhist Religion in China, from the time of its introduction into that country. [Principally memoirs of Translators.] 6 Volumes; 13 Kiouen.

Suh-kao-seng-chou'en.

A connected history of the same kind as the former, published during the Tang dynasty. 12 Volumes; 40 Kiouen.

Nan-hae-ki-kwei-chou'en.

Records concerning visits and returns to the Southern Seas.

An interesting account of Buddhism in India and Ceylon, &c. 2 Volumes; 4 Kiouen.

LXXVII.

Sung-Kao-seng-chuen.

Account of the chief Priests of the Buddhist Religion; composed during the Sung dynasty, 988 A.D. 12 Volumes; 30 Kiouen.

Wu-king.

Five Sûtras, as follows:—

(*a*) **Ping-sha-wang-wu-un-king.**

The five vows of Bimbasara raja.

(*b*) **Lieou-li-wang-king.**

Vaiduryarâja Sûtra.

(*c*) **Fo-shwo-hae-pah-te-king.**

Buddha declares the eight excellences of the Sea.

(*d*) **Fo-shwo-fa-hae-king.**

Buddha delivers the Sûtra called Fa-hai, *i.e.*, Sea of the Law.

(*e*) **Fo-shwo-i-tsuh-king.**

Buddha declares the Sûtra called the wonders or sufficiency of Truth.

Translated by a Upasakawa, of the Wu dynasty.

Fa-hien-chouen.

The travels of Fa-hien. 1 Volume; pp. 34.

Pi-ku-ni-chouen.

Memoirs of celebrated Bhikunis, or female mendicants.

Compiled by Pao-chang, of the Tsin dynasty. 1 Volume; 4 Kiouen.

Fa-tsa-iu-song-king.

Sûtra containing a miscellaneous collection of choice stanzas from the Law (Dharma.)

This seems to be another version of the Dharmapada; composed by Dhwmatrâta, and translated during the Sung dynasty. It is without the fables or avadanas, and is all in verse. 1 Volume; 33 Sections (vargas.)

Po-tse-lun.

A discourse on the confutation of heresy.

Compiled during the Tang dynasty, by a Shaman called Fa-lin. 1 Volume; 2 Parts; pp. 27 and 28.

(*a*) Fo-pan-ni-pan-king.

The Parinirvâna Sûtra.

This appears to be the same as the Sutra known in the South; and partly translated by G. Turnour. It was translated into Chinese by a Shaman, called Fa-tsu, of the Western Tsin dynasty, *circ.* 200 A.D. pp. 28 and 28; 2 Parts.

(*b*) Yin-pen-yuh-sing-king.

The Sutra which explains the birth of desire (lust) in a man's (heart.)

Translated by 'An-shi-kao, of the after Han dynasty, pp. 16.

(*c*) Fo-shwo-fan-kang-luh-shi-i-kin-king.

Buddha speaks of the 62 heretical views combatted in the Brahmajâla Sutra.

Translated by a Upasikawa, of the Wu period. pp. 24.

(*d*) Fo-shwo-shi-kia-lo-yueh-luh-fang-lai-king.

Buddha recites the history of a person called Sigâla (vada), bowing to the six quarters of space.

Translated by 'An-shi-kao, of the after Han dynasty, pp. 9.

(*a*) Shi-men-pin-kan-lun.

(*b*) Pin'g-ching-lun.

Two treatises, in 1 Volume. The first, "On ten methods of instruction in which logical distinctions are to be observed." (?) The second is a discourse about Bimbasara raja. Both belonging to the Tang dynasty.

LXXVIII.

Sz-pi-shwui-ch'an-fa.

A religious service called "The Laws or Rules which regulate the Confessional Service called the Washing, or Water of the merciful and compassionate (one)," or "The merciful and compassionate Washing or Baptism."

[A singular service, containing expressions similar to those found in use elsewhere.] In 1 Volume; 3 Parts; with a Preface by the Emperor Yung-loh. (Ming dynasty.)

Sz-pi-taeu-yang-chan-fa.

Rules for the Service called the Altar or Religious precinct of the merciful and compassionate one.

A work without date or author's name. In 3 Volumes; 10 Kiouen (chapters.)

Wu-pan-tung-pen.

Five separate confessionals (under different names.) In 1 Volume.

Composed principally by the Tien-tai Priests, during the Sung dynasty.

1 Volume; 5 Kiouen. [There are three other Volumes, numbered A. B. C. on the covers, containing confessional Services and dhârani under different names; composed chiefly by Priests of the Tien-chu Temple at Tien-tai.]

Lih-tai-san-pao-ki.

Records concerning the "three gems" (triratna), during successive generations.

This work, in 5 Volumes, and 15 Kiouen, contains a general history of the Buddhist succession, and of Books published during each period. Dates from the Tsui dynasty, 590 A.D.

Ta-Tang-Si-yu-ki.

This is the well known work compiled by Hiouen Thsang.

It is in 3 Volumes, and 12 Kiouen. It dates from the Tang dynasty.

U-fa-lun.

A treatise on "The preservation of the Law," or "In defence of Dharma."

Seems to be a controversial work, written by a householder (layman) called Chang-shang-ying, of the Sung dynasty. 1 Volume.

Pien-ching-lun.

A discourse on "The distinction of Truth," or, "On the way of distinguishing the Truth."

A controversial work, in 3 Volumes, and 9 Kiouen. Edited by a Shaman called Shi-fa-lin, of the Tang dynasty.

LXXIX.

Luh-tsu-fa-pao-tan-king.

Teachings of the six (Chinese) Patriarchs. 1 Volume; pp. 72.

Chou'en-fa-ching-tsung-ki.

Records of the Histories of the various Patriarchs.

This History is valuable. It includes a memoir of each of the 28 Indian Buddhist Patriarchs, and of the six Chinese do. 3 Volumes 10 Kiouen.

Chouen-fa-ching-tsung-lun.

This seems to be a treatise on the subject of the preceding work. 1 Volume; 2 parts; pp. 16 and 21.

Tsung-men-leu-iu-suh-ts'a.

A connected history of Buddhist doctrine in India and China. 7 Volumes; 22 Kiouen

King-tih-chouen-tang-lu.

Literally, a catalogue or index of the history of eminent Buddhist Priests, which may act as a lamp.

A history of Buddhism, from the time of Kâsyapa Buddha, downwards. 9 Volumes; 30 Kiouen.

Ming-hioh-shan-sse-wu-lu.

A connected account of the sayings of the Master Ming-hioh, belonging to the Contemplative School.

In 2 Volumes; 6 Kiouen. [There is some confusion, however, in the Titles of these two Volumes.]

LXXX.

Ta-hwui-hioh-shan-sse-p'ho-shwo.

The 'dicta' or 'utterances' of the Master Ta-hwui-hioh, belonging to the Shan or Contemplative School. 5 Books; 5 Kiouen.

Ta-hwui-p'ho-hioh-shan-sse-wu-lu.

An arranged digest of the sayings of Ta-hwui-p'ho-hioh (whose likeness is given on the first page of the Book), of the Shan or Contemplative School. 3 Volumes; 12 Kiouen.

Un-wu-kwo-shan-sse-wu-lu.

An orderly digest of the sayings of Un-wu-kwo, belonging to the Shan School. 6 Volumes; 20 Kiouen.

Fu-kiau-pien.

Extracts from the teachings of Fu-kiau. (?) 1 Volume; 2 Parts.

Ta-hwui-shu-man.

Questions relating to the Books of Ta-hwui-p'ho-hioh. 1 Volume.

Ta-hwui-fa-wu.

Religious conversations or remarks of Ta-hwui. 1 Volume.

Chung-fung-ho-shang-kwang-lu.

An Index to the opinions of (Tien-Muh), a Priest of Chung-fung [or, of the Priests of the Tien-Muh-chung-fung Monastery.] 8 Volumes.

LXXXI.

Miau-fa-lien-hwa-king-un-i.

Abstruse doctrines of the Saddharma pundarika Sûtra. 10 Volumes; 10 Kiouen; by Che-tche, of Tien Tai.

Fa-hwa-un-i-shi-cha.

Another work similar to the preceding, by a Shaman of Tien-tai. 10 Volumes; 10 Kiouen

Miau-fa-lien-hwa-king-wan-ku.

Extracts from the same work, by Che-tche, of Tien-tai. 10 Volumes, viz., Kiouen 1 to Kiouen 10.

Chung-fung-ho-shang-kwang-lu.

An exposition by a Tien-tai Priest, called Chung-Fung. 4 Volumes.

LXXXII.

Fa-hwa-man-keu-ki.

Records concerning the sentences of the Saddharma Pundarika. A work of the Chinese Tien-t'ai School. 12 Volumes.

Mo-ho-chi-kwan.

The doctrine of Samata (discipline), and Vipasyana (contemplation), according to the Great Vehicle. [These two stages are supposed to be the essential parts of Buddhism, both in the lesser and greater developments] By Tien-t'ai (Tche-che.) 10 Volumes.

LXXXIII.

Chi-kwan-foo-hing-chou'en-hwang-keue.

A voluminous work on the two stages of Samata (rest leading to knowledge), and Vipasyana (contemplation.) Published during the Tang dynasty. 15 Volumes; 40 Kiouen.

LXXXIV.

Kwan-yin-un-i-ki.

Records respecting the Esoteric Teaching of Kwan-yin (Avalokiteswara.) 2 Volumes; 4 Kiouen.

Pu-sah-kiai-i-lau.

Remarks on the character of the Rules that relate to the conduct of Bôdhisatwas. By Che-tche, of Tien-tai. 1 Volume; 2 Parts; pp. 31 and 34.

Kwan-yin-un-i.

Esoteric doctrine of Kwan-yin. By Che-tche, of Tien-tai. 1 Volume; 2 Parts; pp. 29 and 31.

Kwan-yin-i-lau.

Remarks on the Esoteric doctrine of Kwan-yin. By Che-tche. 1 Volume; 2 Parts; pp. 34 and 38.

Kwan-yin-i-lau-ki.

Records on some parts of the Esoteric doctrine of Kwan-yin. 2 Volumes; 4 Kiouen.

Kwan-wou-liang-sheu-Fo-king-lau.

Remarks on the Amitâbha Sûtra. By Che-tche. 1 Volume; pp. 31.

Kwan-wou-liang-sheu-miu-tsung-chau.

Notices extracted from the Tsung School, respecting the Amîtâbha Sûtra. By Che-tai, of the Sung dynasty. 2 Volumes; 6 Kiouen.

Tsing-kwan-yin-king-lau.

Remarks on the Kwan-yin-king. By Che-tche. 1 Volume; pp. 34.

Che-tche-ta-sse-shan-men-hau-kieuh.

Last records of Che-tche, respecting the teaching of the Shan (contemplative) School. 1 Volume; pp. 12.

Tsing-kwan-yin-king-lau-chen-i-ch'au.

Explanations and collected remarks on the teaching of the Tsing-kwan-yin-sûtra. By a Shaman of the Sung dynasty, called Che-un. 2 Volumes; 4 Kiouen.

Heo-i-san-mui.

A work of the Mahâ Prajna paramita class, on Samadhi. By Che-tai. 1 Volume; pp. 35.

Sze-nien-chu.

Four Memorable Treatises or considerations. By Che-tche. 1 Volume; 4 Kiouen.

Kin-kwang-ming-man-ku-ki.

Records on some passages from the Suvarna prabhâsa Sûtra. By Che-tai, of the Sung dynasty. 6 Volumes; 6 Kiouen; 12 Parts.

Kin-kwong-ming-wan-ku.

Extracts from the Suvarna prabhâsa Sûtra. By Che-tche, of Tien-tai. 2 Volumes; 6 Kiouen.

LXXXV.

Ta-pan-ni-pan-king-lo.

Comments on the Mahâparinirvana Sûtra. By Chang-'an, of the Tsui dynasty. In 10 Volumes; 33 Kiouen.

Ta-pan-ni-pan-king-un-i.

The secret or mysterious doctrines of the Mahâparinirvana Sûtra. By a Tien-tai Priest, called Kun-teng (the anointed or consecrated.) In 1 Volume; 2 Parts; pp. 27 and 28.

Kin-kwong-ming-king-un-i-shih-wei-ki.

A collection of forgotten comments on the mysterious parts of the *Suvarna prabhasa Sutra*. By a Shaman called "Chi-tai," of the Sung dynasty. 2 Volumes; 6 Kiouen.

Kin-kwong-ming-king-un-i.

Mysterious or secret wisdom of the Suvarna prabhasa Sutra. By the celebrated 'Che-tche,' of Tien-tai, who flourished during the Tsui dynasty, 580 A.D. 1 Volume; 2 Parts; pp. 20 and 21.

Chi-kwan-tso-shan-fa-iu.

This is the famous work known as *Siu-chi-kwan*. It is a Treatise by *Che-tche*, of *Tien-tai*, on the two duties or practices known as *Chi* (Samata), and *Kwan* (Vipasyana) Date as before. 1 Volume; pp. 49.

Chi-kwan-i-li.

Rules for practising the above duties of Samata and Vipasyana. By a Tien-tai Priest. 1 Volume; pp. 44.

Fa-hwa-king-'an-luh-hing-i.

A commentary on the meaning of a particular section of the *Saddharma pundarika* Sutra. Written by a Priest (belonging to the Meditative School), in the Tsui dynasty. 1 Volume; pp. 19.

Chu-fa-wu-tsing-san-mui-fa-men.

Rules for the practice of Samâdhi. By a Priest (Shan-sse) called Sz'-tai, of the Tsui dynasty. 1 Volume; 2 Parts; pp. 21 and 30.

Fa-un-ki-iu [or, more fully,] Ni-pan-un-i-fah-un-ki-iu.

Comments on the Parinirvâna Sûtra. By a Shaman, 'Chi-un, of the Sung dynasty. 2 Volumes; 4 Kiouen.

Ta-shing-chi-kwan-fa-men.

Rules for practising the two duties of Samata and Vipasyana, according to the Great Vehicle. By a Priest (Shan-sse) called Sz'-tai, of the Tsui dynasty. 1 Volume; 4 Parts; pp. 84.

(a) Kin-kong-po-ye-king-lo.

Comments on the Vajrachchedika Sutra. By a Tien-tai Priest.

(b) Tien-tai-sz-kiai-i.

Explanations of the four principal modes of instruction adopted by Tien-tai (*i.e.*, Che-tche, of Tien-tai.) 1 Volume; pp. 21; pp. 28.

LXXXVI.

[Contains 20 Volumes; all connected with the Tien-Tai School of Native Chinese Buddhists, and, therefore, of small interest as belonging to the Tripitaka.]

LXXXVII.

Fa-yan-king-lew.

Hangings or ornaments of the Avatamsaka Sûtra [Chinese compilation.] 18 Volumes; 60 Kiouen.

LXXXVIII.

Fa-yan-king-tsui-lu-hin-i-luh.

Notes and comments on the Avatamsaka Sûtra.

A compilation of a priest of the Ta-fa-yen Temple, in the Tsing-ling Hill, called Tang-kwan—Tang dynasty. 15 Volumes, from Kiouen 1 to Kiouen 50.

LXXXIX.

Fa-yan-king-tsui-lau-hin-i-ch'au.

Native (Chinese) comments on the teachings of the Avatamsaka Sûtra. 12 Volumes, numbering from Kiouen 51 to Kiouen 90.

XC.

Yih-tsai-king-yin-i.

The meanings of all the words used throughout the Sûtras, with their sounds. 8 Volumes; 26 Kiouen; by Yuen-ying, of the Tang dynasty.

Shaou-tien-tai-tsang-yin.

Sounds of all words used throughout the Sacred Books (Pitakas.) By a Shaman of the Sung dynasty, named Chu-kwan. 1 Volume.

Fa-yan-king-yin-i.

Sounds of words found in the Avatamsaka Sûtra. 1 Volume; by a Shaman of the Tang dynasty.

Fa-yan-fen-tsai-chang.

Divisions and sections of the Avatamsaka. 2 Volumes; by a Shaman of the Tang dynasty, called Fa-tsong. 4 Kiouen.

Pan-jo-sin-king-lin-chu-ki.

Records concerning the Prajnahridaya Sûtra. 1 Volume; 2 Parts.

(a) Yu-lan-pwan-king-chau.

Remarks on the Avalambin Sutra.

The Sûtra is first given as it was translated by Chu-fa-hu (the Indian Dharmaraksha), of the Western Tsin dynasty. The remarks or comments then follow.

(b) Kin-sse-tseu-chang.

A section of the Avatamsaka Sûtra, called the "Golden Lion."

(c) Fo-shwo-O-mi-to-king-lau.

Comments on the Amitâbha Sûtra. [The three preceding in 1 Volume.]

Fo-hien-kiau-king-tsih-iu.

Comments on the Sûtra called "The dying instructions of Buddha." 1 Volume; by Kumârajiva (translator.)

(a) Fa-yan-king-chi-kwai.

References to the Avatamsaka Sûtra, by a Shaman of the Tang dynasty.

(b) Fa-kai-kwan-men.

Explanations of a Section of the Avatamsaka Sutra, called 'Fa-kai-kwan-men.' The preceding, (a) and (b), form 1 Volume.

(a) Fa-yan-san-pao-chang.

A section of the Avatamsaka, called 'san-pao' (three gems.)

(b) Another section of the Avatamsaka.

(c) Un-jin-lun.

A discourse on the origin of things, and of man. [The three preceding in 1 Volume.]

(a) Fa-kai-un-keng.

A discourse on the Fa-kai section of the Avatamsaka Sutra.

(b) Pan-jo-sin-king-leuh-lau.

Brief notices of the Prajnahridaya Sutra. [The two preceding form 1 Volume.]

XCI.

Tsui-chung-king-muh-lu.

A catalogue of Buddhist Books existing in China during the Tsui dynasty. 5 Volumes; 6 Kiouen.

Chi-yuen-fa-pao-kha'n-tung-tsung-lu.

A comparative list of Buddhist Books existing in China during the period Chi-yuen, Tang dynasty. 4 Volumes; 10 Kiouen.

[This is the work on which *Julien* founds his *Sin. Sanse. Concordance.*]

Lang-ka-king-chu-kiai.

Explanations of the Laukâvatara Sutra. 4 Volumes; 4 Kiouen.

Wu-chow-kai-teng-chung-king-mu-lu.

An Index of Sacred Books of the period "Wu-chow." 5 Volumes; 14 Kiouen.

Pien-wei-lu.

The catalogue of Pien-wei. (Seems to be a Taouist work.) 2 Volumes; 5 Kiouen.

Ta-tsang-shing-kiau-pao-piu-mu.

Another catalogue, of the Yuen period. 4 Volumes; 10 Kiouen.

(*a*) Sin-king-chu-kiai.

Explanations of the (Prajna)hridaya Sutra.

(*b*) Kin-kong-king-chu-kiai.

Explanations of the Vajrachhedika Sutra.

(*c*) Some imperial verses in praise of the above.

[The preceding form 1 Volume.]

XCII.

Tchu-fo-shai-tsun-shin-sang-ming-king.

Names of all the Buddhas.

This work seems to contain the names of all the fabulous Buddhas, invented in the course of the development of the system. 12 Volumes; 40 Kiouen.

Tchu-Fo-shai-tsun-ming-chung-kiuh-ho.

Stanzas in praise of all the Buddhas. 4 Volumes; 10 Kiouen. [The rest in Case 93.]

XCIII.

Tchu-Fo-shai-tsun-ming-ching-kiuh-ho.

Verses in praise of the names of all the Buddhas, continued from *Case* 92, from Kiouen 11 to Kiouen 50, inclusive. No author's name. A work of Chinese Buddhism.

Shin-tsang-tch'uen.

Records of Holy Priests.

Brief memoirs of the principal translators of the Indian works brought to China. 3 Volumes; 9 Kiouen. (A Chinese work.)

Kan-ying-kiuh-ho.

A supplementary Volume of hymns or ditties in honor of Buddha. 16 pp.

XCIV.

Ta-Ming-san-tsong-fa-su.

An extensive treatise, containing a series of explanations of Buddhist terms arranged numerically, or rather, an explanation of all numerical terms in the Buddhist Tripitaka. The phrases extend from 1 (*i.e.*, phrases beginning with *one*) up to 84,000.

In 20 Volumes; 50 Chapters. Compiled by various Shamans of Upper India.

XCV.

Sheu-leng-yan-hwui-kiai.

Collected comments on the Surangama Sutra. By various Chinese Priests. 6 Volumes.

Fa-yan-un-tan-hwui-un-ki.

Records of notices and observations made on the Avatamsaka Sutra. 12 Volumes; 40 Kiouen.

Fa-hwa-iu-kiai.

Select explanations of the Saddharma pundarika Sûtra. 7 Volumes; 7 Kiouen.

XCVI.

Yuen-hioh-leuh-chau.

Comments on the writings of Yuen-hioh. (Chinese.) Altogether, with others of the same nature, 16 Volumes.

Shiu-lun-san-chau.

Comments on the writings of the Priests of a district called Shiu-hing-fu, near Canton. 3 Volumes.

[This case contains some other Volumes, of Chinese origin, on esoteric Buddhism, of no importance.]

XCVII.

Shih-kin-kong-king-k'han-teng-ki.

Records concerning the Vajrach'hedika Sutra. (A Chinese work.) 3 Volumes; 7 Kiouen.

Kin-kong-king-lau-lun-tswan-iu.

Collected discourses and notes on the Vajrach'hedika Sutra. 1 Volume; 2 Parts. (A Chinese work.)

Kiau-shing-fa-sho.

Matters of doctrine arranged numerically. (A useful terminological dictionary.) 8 Books; 8 Kiouen.

Sse-kiau-i-tsi-chu.

Mixed explanations of the truths of the four Schools of (Buddhist) teaching. (The four Schools are those explained in the Catechism of the Shamans (glossary). 1. The Little Vehicle. 2 and 3. Two developments of the Greater Vehicle. 4. The conciliation of the two Vehicles in the Madhyamika School.

By Tien-tai (Tche-chi.) 3 Volumes.

Wei-Mo-king-chu.

Explanations of the Vimalakirtti Sutra.

(A Chinese work.) 5 Volumes; 10 Kiouen. [This is a valuable exegesis of the Sutra, with verbal explanations.]

Hwa-yan-un-jin-lun.

A discourse on a Section of the Avatamsaka Sutra, on the origin of man. 2 Volumes; 3 Parts.

Che-i-lun.

A discourse on the eradication of unbelief. (A Chinese work.) 1 Volume; 5 Kiouen.

[This is a work well deserving attention, and full of pithy aphorisms.]

XCVIII.

Fo-tsu-tung-ch'au.

A complete history of the Buddhist Patriarchs (and of the Religion generally.) 16 Volumes; 90 Kiouen. [Chinese compilation.]

Shau-lin-pa'o-shun.

Precious extracts from the School of Contemplative Buddhists. 1 Volume.

XCIX.

Fan-tsi-ming-i-ts'a.

Restoration of Sanscrit words to their true meaning.

This is the Book alluded to by *Julien* in his "Méthode," and is a work of great use in the restoration of Sanscrit sentences. 7 Volumes; 20 Kiouen.

Ta-fang-kwang-fu-hwa-yan-king-lau-ch'au.

Comments on the Avatamsaka Sûtra, of the Vaipulya class. 9 Volumes; 29 Kiouen.

C.

Tsze-men-king-shun.

Directions for lay disciples. 4 Volumes.

Shan-tsung-ching-wing.

Extracts from the teachings of the Shan School (contemplative sect) 9 Volumes 20 Kiouen.

San-kiau-ping-sin-lun.

A Chinese treatise on the three methods of Instruction, 1 Volume; 3 Parts.

Kin-lu-man-ts'a.

Miscellaneous records concerning the doctrine of Buddha. 5 Volumes; 19 Kiouen.

Pih-chang-tsing-kwei.

A work on Chinese Buddhism. 2 Volumes; 4 Kiouen.

CI.

Suh-chou'en-teng-lu.

A connected account of eminent Teachers of the Contemplative School of Buddhism in China. 7 Volumes; 21 Kiouen.

Lien-tsung-pa'o-lam.

Another work of the same character. 3 Volumes; 10 Kiouen.

Wan-shen-tung-kwai-tsa.

3 Volumes; 3 Parts. (Literally) Ten-thousand excellences, the same (one) return (refuge); a miscellany.

Shan-un-chou-chu-tsa.

Comments and explanations of the doctrines of the Contemplative School; a miscellany. 1 Volume.

Pah-shi-kwai-keu.

Regulations, or Rules, on the square, respecting the 8 kinds of knowledge, viz., eye-knowledge, ear-knowledge, nose-knowledge, tongue-knowledge, body-knowledge, thought-knowledge, mona- (manas) knowledge, a-la-ye knowledge; (*i.e.*, the knowledge, as it is called, of the eighth viscera. *Vid. Cat. of Ch. Bud. Appendix.*) 1 Volume.

Hwang-pih-chouen-sin-fa-iu.

Traditions and teachings of Priests of the Hwang-pih Hill, or monastery. 1 Volume.

Three Volumes containing dhârani and obscure explanations of the Shan sect. Numbered on cover, L. M. N.

CII.

Ku-tsun-suh-wu-lu.

Sayings of the old worthies (of the Shan or Contemplative School.) 12 Volumes; 48 Chapters (Kiouen.)

Suh-chou'en-tang-lu.

A connected history of eminent men of the Shan or Contemplative Sect.

CIII.

Shan-tsung-song-ku-leen-chu-tung-ts'a.

A connected series of chants or gathas, belonging to the Shan or Contemplative School of Buddhists. [This is a miscellaneous record of all the Patriarchs belonging to this School.] 10 Volumes; 40 Kiouen.

Fo-tsu-lew-ki.

Occasional records respecting the Buddhist Patriarchs, 15 Volumes; 54 Kiouen.

ADDENDA.

Omitted from Case XXXI.

Tsa-A-han-king.

The Samyuktâgama Sutra. 15 Volumes; 50 Kiouen. Translated by Gunabhadra, of the Sung dynasty. [Deserves careful examination.]

Omitted from Case XXXVI.

Shi-kia-p'ho.

A life of Sâkya (Buddha).

This work, which is in ten Kiouen (books) and thirty-four chapters, is a compilation made by a priest Sang-yau, of the Tse dynasty, *circ.* 470 A.D., from valuable books in the Buddhist Canon (particularly the Dirghâgama Sutra), respecting the personal history of Sâkya. [It deserves a distinct analysis.]

Shi-kia-fang-chi.

A history or record of the regions or country of Sâkya (Buddha).

This work contains a compendious history of countries in India—derived, as it would seem, principally from Hiouen Thsang. It was compiled by Shi-tau-i, of the Tang dynasty. It is in two books and eight parts. [Deserves analysis.]

Shi-kia-shi-p'ho.

History or memoirs of the family of Sâkya (Buddha).

Contains the names of Sâkya's ancestors, and also events in his own family history. Compiled by Shi-tau-i, of the Tang dynasty, from the Buddhist Canon. [Deserves attention.]

Omitted from Case LXIII.

Wu-lun.

Five short treatises or Shasters.

(*a*) Kiai-shin-tsuh-lun.

Dhatukayapada, by the Venerable Vasumitra. Translated by Hiouen Tsang, of the Tang dynasty.

(*b*) Wou-sse-pi-po-sha-lun.

Pantchakarma vibasha Shastra. (?)

Composed by the Venerable Dharmatrata, and translated by Hiouen Thsang.

(*c, d, e*)—Three Treatises on the origin and history of the different Schools of Buddhism. The first is anonymous; the second and third are by the Venerable Vasumitra. These Treatises have been used by M. Wassilief *(Bouddisme, pp. 222, ss.)* in his essay on "Differences of opinion"—*(deuxieme supplement.)*

Omitted from Case LXV.

(*a*) **Ta-shing-fa-kai-wou-tsa-pieh-lun.**

A treatise by Sthiramati Bodhisatwa, and translated into Chinese during the Tang dynasty.

(*b*) **Kin-kong-teng-yu-kia-chung-fah-Po-ti-sin-lun.**

A work on Yoga. Translated by Amogha during the Tang dynasty.

(*c*) **Ying-sho-chi-lun.**

This is an important work, and deserves examination. It appears to have been composed so late as the Yuen dynasty, by one called Sze-pa, and translated by Sha-lo-pa. It contains an account of the Buddhist mythology, and also of its history under successive Kings in India, Kashmir, &c. Vid. Part I., p. 20, ss.

Omitted from Case LXVIII.

(*a*) **Shiau-hing-pen-hi-king.**

This is an old Life of Buddha, in seven Chapters; translated by Kong-Mang-tsiang and another, during the after Han dynasty. Deserves attention.

(*b*) **Ta-tseu-sui-ying-pen-hi-king.**

This is another brief memoir of Buddha (Kumâra), dating from the Wu period, *circ.* 170 A.D., and very interesting.

COMPENDIOUS REPORT ON THE FOREGOING CATALOGUE.

It is evident from an examination of the books named in the previous pages, that the Buddhist Canon, as it is accepted in China and Japan, is not a trustworthy guide to what was the ancient "Rule" of that Faith. The Canou in fact consists of a *congeries* of different works, admitted, in an arbitrary way, by the successive Emperors who patronized the faith, into the number of Sacred Books. Hence we are prepared to find treatises of different kinds and widely-varying dates, ranking together as parts of a continuous System. In fact, whatever books were brought to China from the date of the introduction of the Buddhist Religion into that country, down to the time of the Emperor *Wan-leih*, who caused copies of translations of these works to be included in the Canon we are considering—such compose the body of this vast and so-called Sacred Literature. In other words, the Canon includes books brought to and translated in China during a period extending from A.D. 70 to A.D. 1600.

But whilst this is the case with respect to the Books in a Collective character, or regarded as a supposed Rule of Faith, we cannot overrate their importance as a guide to a comprehensive knowledge of Buddhism throughout all its stages of development. It is hardly necessary to say that Primitive Buddhism, as it came from the hands of its Founder, rapidly underwent changes, or, to use the ordinary word, expanded, through successive ages, into Systems of Belief and of external worship or Ritual, widely differing from one another; so that, when speaking or writing of this Faith and its present position in the comparative list of religions, we cannot confine our remarks to the earliest writings or the small area over which the purer, because more primitive, form of Belief is diffused, for this would lead to no knowledge of the mode in which it grew into its present multiple form, or the secret of the power it has exercised over the minds of so many differing populations. In fact it is evident that whilst Buddhism retains in all its aspects the same basis of moral truth, and is generally marked by the same thread of philosophical speculation, yet it has been able to accommodate itself, by its facile and unresisting spirit, to the genius of people differing in all the outward phases of civilization, and in every stage of national development. Hence its wonderful advance and outspread; and hence the differing forms in which it presents itself to us in Thibet, Mongolia, China and Ceylon.

The books in this catalogue may be classed generally, and for the sake of brevity, under the heads Vinaya, Sûtra, Abhidharma, and Miscellaneous. Under the first we have the rules for the Priesthood and the Nuns, according to all the schools. In Case XLII. are the Sarvastavadavinaya and the Xi-kie-mo; that is, Rules of discipline according to the school of the Sarvastavadins. In Case XLII. are similar rules according to the school of the Dharmaguptas (the most prevalent in China). In Case XLV. we have the Vinaya Pitaka, as known in the Mulasarvastivadina and the Mahisasika schools; the latter said to prevail in Ceylon under the name or title of Sammatiyas. In the succeeding cases there is a large collection of works treating on the subject of discipline in every school. In Case XLVIII. are various works of the Vinaya class, bearing the name Mâtrikâ. This title, or the class of books bearing this title, is alluded to by Burnouf (*Introduction* p. 48), and considered by him as equivalent to ABHIDHARMA, although he refers to Mr. Turnour's remark that "the works called the Mâtrikâ belong to the Vinaya." In the Chinese books before us there can be no doubt as to this point, the second work in the Case above named is distinctly termed "Vinaya Mâtrikâ," according to the school of the Sarvastavadins. On examining this and corresponding works belonging to other schools, I find they are occupied in solving various cases of conscience, involving transgression against the Rules of the Pratimoksha; *i.e.*, in determining the character and amount of guilt attaching to different sinful actions;—some of the sections are of the grossest possible character, alluding to cases of extreme turpitude, and relating instances of such conduct, and Buddha's judgment thereon. It is quite unnecessary to cite passages from these works, as their character may be surmised from what has been said. At the beginning of the "Pi-ni-mu-lun," *i.e.*, the Vinaya Mâtrikâ Shastra, the reason given for the use of the term Matrika, is, "that these works are intended to exercise a *motherly* part toward both Bikshus and Bikshunis."

Under this division of VINAYA, as will be seen from the catalogue, are works referring to the conduct of the lay disciples (Upasikawas), as well as of the Novice (Samanera). I find that most of the works alluded to in Mr. A. Csoma Korosi's analysis of the Thibetan Dulva* are contained in the catalogue (whilst it includes very many not named by him), and his remarks agree in the main with the contents of such of these as I have been able to examine for the purpose of comparison. It would be of the utmost service towards a precise knowledge of the different tenets of the schools if some of these works were carefully analyzed or fully translated. On comparing Mr. Dickson's translation of the Pratimoksha (J.R A.S., Oct., 1875) with those contained in Case XLVIII., I find that the Pali version agrees most accurately with the copy known as *'Ng-fen-kiai-pen, i e.*, the Pratimoksha used in the Mahisasika school, and this in connection with remarks made by the author of a work found in Case LXXVI., Nan-hae-ki-kwei-chou'en, who states expressly that the Buddhists of Ceylon are Sammatiyas, and with Fa-hien's remark, Chap. XL., that his copy of the Vinaya, procured in Ceylon, belonged to the Mahisasika school, makes it probable that the Buddhist literature of that country belongs chiefly to the school so named.

With respect to the second division of the Canon coming under the name of Sutra, it would be impossible to enter into details. There are several thousand of such works (great and small) in the collection, and to attempt to give even a bare outline of these, would require the labour of many years. The four Agamas, as referred to in Cases XXIX , XXX., and XXXI , are of great interest, as they seem to correspond with the four-fold division known in the South; if this is so, the DIRGHAGAMA (Case XXXI.), represents the Digha-nikaya, or, Book of long Suttas; the Madyamagama (Case XXIX.), agrees with the Majjhima-nikaya, or, middle-sized Sutras; the Tsa-A-han-king (omitted from Case XXXI., Vid. *Addenda*), or, Samyuktagama, with the Sanyutta-nikâya, or, groups of Suttas; and the Tsang-yih-A-han-king (Case XXX.), with the Anguttara-nikâya, or, Suttas of eminence. It is to be remarked, however, with respect to the last named, that the explanation given of the Title is, that the compilations included therein are of a general character, and arranged *numerically*.

From an examination of the four Agamas, we find that they consist of short Sutras delivered by Buddha at different times, and in various places; and from the size of the collection it is not improbable that they may include as many as the 17,575 Suttas said to be comprised in the Nikâyas before named. It would be highly interesting if a list of the contents of these respective volumes could be secured for the sake of comparison.

The SUTRAS in the catalogue are easily distinguished into two great classes—the primitive and more authentic agreeing in the main with those in the Southern school, and the later or expanded ones, peculiar to the North.

Among the first we may mention the following (Case LXXVII.): *Fo-pan-ni-pan-king*, the Parinirvana Sutra; this agrees with the translation from the Southern work of the same name, the text of which has already been published in the Journal of the Royal Asiatic Society, and a partial translation many years ago given by Mr. G. Turnour in the Bengal Branch of the same Society. It will be interesting when a full translation from the Pali is before us—to publish side by side with it one from this Chinese version of the same Sutta. The comparatively early date of the version in our catalogue (about A.D. 200) is quite in accordance with what we should expect.

The Sutra lettered *c* in the same case, and called *Fo-shwo-tan-kang-luh-shi-i-kiu-king*, is, I find, a version of the Brahmajala Sutra, as it is known in the South; it has been partly translated by Mr. Gogerly (Ceylon Friend). There are differences in the versions, but of no great moment, and it is satisfactory to find that the agreement between them is so marked as it is.

The next Sutra in the same case, and lettered *d*, is also an interesting one. It is a version of the Sigala Sutra, or, as it is known in the South, the Sigalovada. In Chinese the title, as given in the catalogue, would make the name of the pious youth "Sigalava;" but *va* is probably a contraction for *vada*.

An English translation of the Southern version of this Sermon has recently appeared from the learned pen of Professor Childers (*Contemporary Review*, February, 1876), and as this

* Asiatic Researches, Volume XX.

publication is easily within reach, I think it would be well to show the similarity of the versions by reproducing a portion of the Chinese copy of the same work in Englis It begins thus—

Fo-shwo-shi-kia-lo-yue-luh-fang-lai-king.

Translated by Gan-shi-kao, of the After Han dynasty, circ. 220 *A.D.*

"Buddha was residing on the Kukuta mountain. At this time there was a noblemar son called Sigalava, who, early in the morning, had arisen to adorn or dress his hair, bathe his body, and put on his comely robes. In such a condition he was, when turnii to the east he made four prostrations, turning to the south he made four prostratior turning to the west he likewise worshipped four times, and turning to the north he did tl same, then looking upwards he four times bent his head, and also looking down at tl earth. Now Buddha at this time was traversing the country begging alms, and as he w going he saw at a distance the youth Sigala thus worshipping. Straightway he repaired the house where he lived, and asked him what religion it was that required these six ac of worship. On this Sigalava said, "whilst my father was alive he taught me thus to ador without explaining the why or wherefore, and now he is dead and gone I cannot dare neglect or forget his instruction."

Buddha said, "your father taught you thus to worship, but not with bodily prostr tions." Immediately Sigalava fell at the feet of Buddha, and entreated him to expla this mental adoration of which he spoke. On this the blessed one replied, "Listen the and ponder what I say in your heart." On this the youth remained silently attentiv Buddha then began, "If a man can observe the four moral rules without transgression, I shall have reverence in this world, and afterwards go to heaven. The first rule is not kill anything that has life. Second, not to steal. Third, not to commit adultery. Fourt not to lie or slander. When once the heart gives way to such evil desire, covetousnes foolish imagination, anger and folly—then, unable to rule itself, from want of prop attention, these evil propensities will daily increase, and the reputation of such a ma decrease as the waning moon. But being able to rule and control himself in the particulars, then the reputation of such a man shall increase as the brightness of tl moon waxing to the fifteenth day of the month, when it becomes full." Again Buddl said, "there are six things that cause a daily diminution of one's substance (wealth 1. Rejoicing to drink wine. 2. Delighting in gambling 3. Sleeping in the morning an getting up towards night. 4. Invitations given and accepted. 5. Associating with wicke companions. 6. Pride and arrogancy towards others. A man who falls into the four sir first named, and walks according to the particulars last given, shall never attain a virtuo reputation and daily shall his substance be frittered away and disappear." And now what a the six prostrations of which we speak? Buddha said, "Of evil companionships there a four sorts: 1. The man who inwardly dislikes you, but outwardly professes friendshi 2. The man who speaks well of you before your face, and slanders you behind your bac 3. The man who, in the time of adversity, is sorrowful before men on your account, b behind your back rejoices and triumphs. 4. The man who outwardly behaves as one the same kin with another, but inwardly is full of hatred and evil thoughts."

There are also four kinds of virtuous friendship. 1. The man who outwardly acts a reprover, but inwardly is full of good wishes and purposes. 2. The man who speal plainly before your face as to your faults, but when away from you speaks only of yo virtues. 3. The man who, during the time of another's sickness, suspends all priva business, in anxiety for the other's recovery. 4. When in the presence of poverty not despise or reject a man on that account, but seriously to consider how to contrive for h friend's advantage and recovery. Again, there are four kinds of evil friendship. 1. man who, from fear of trouble in exhorting another to a virtuous life, lets him go witho reproof into the worst company. 2. A man who instructs another to avoid the compar of the young debauchee, but lets him drink wine with the old profligate. 3. Who teach another to hoard up uselessly, for himself alone, much substance. 4. Who teaches anoth that because he has good friends, he must look down with contumely on those below hir Again, there are four kinds of friendship highly commendable. 1. That of one wh seeing his friend in poverty and distress, bends himself to the work of planning a mode retrenchment. 2. Who will have no "words" with his friend. 3. Who leaves his friend house at Sundown. 4. Who, whether lying down or rising up, is always planning som good thing for his friend. [And so on.]

We may gather from these remarks, that the Sûtras which were translated at an early period in China, were of the same character as those known in Ceylon, and perhaps written in Magadhî.

Other interesting subjects of comparison under the division we are now considering, are the numerous copies of the Dharmapada found in the Northern Collection, with that known in the South. We find in CASE LXVII., p. 87, a work, "*Fa-keu-pi-hu-king*," *i.e.*, comparisons attached to the verses of the Law; in other words, the Avadânas or Fables connected with the Dhammapada. In the same CASE, p. 88, we find a work, *Fa-keu-king*, *i.e.*, the Dhammapada itself. In CASE LXVI., p. 85, there is a work, Ch'uh-yau-king, which turns out to be an expanded copy of the Dhammapada with the accompanying Avadânas. The Title last named signifies in Chinese the "Coming forth of light," or, "The Dawn," and the Preface distinctly states that this is the old meaning of the word "Avadâna."

These several copies of this interesting work may deserve some little notice. We will take the *Fa-keu-king*, found in Case LXVII., first. It is satisfactory to find the following remark at the beginning of the Introduction to this Book.

"The work called 'Tan-poh-keih' (Dhammapada Verses, or, Verses (gathas) of the Dhammapada (Tan-po is the *Phonetic* form of Dhammapada)) consists of choicest selections from all the Sutras. The word 'Tan' means 'The Law' (Dharma), and the word 'Poh' means "verses" or "quotations" (pada), and, therefore, the whole word signifies "verses or quotations from the Law." There are several compilations bearing this name—there is one embracing 900 gathas; another, 700 gathas; another, 500 gâthas. Now the word "gatha," simply means a verse occurring in one of the Sûtras. These verses or utterances were not made at one time, but as occasion prompted; they were delivered by Buddha, and are scattered throughout the 12 different classes of Books comprising the Canon, but particularly in the four Agamas, and they are called Fa-keu (Dhammapada) because they are all to be found in the Books of the Law. The present work consists of 39 Sections, and includes 752 Sections."

On comparing the contents of the Chinese book with the Southern version, known to us through the translation by V. Fausböll and Max Muller, I find that the first eight sections of the Chinese, and the last four (with one other, No. 33), do not occur in the Southern copy. But from No. 9 to No. 35 (with the one exception of 33) the order and contents of the two works are the same. The first eight chapters are named as follows 1. Impermanency (Anitya). 2. The doctrine of the enlightened. 3. The Sravaka 4. Sincere faith. 5. Dutiful attention (or, attention to duty). 6. Consideration 7. Loving kindness. 8. Conversation. The 33rd Section is on "generosity;" the 36th on Nirvâna; 37th, on "Birth and Death;" 38th, on "the advantage of Religion;" and the 39th "on Good Fortune, or, Success."

Comparing the Sections that seem to agree in the South and North, there are some differences, but in the main they are alike.

Let us take a few lines from Chapter II. in the Southern version, which corresponds with Chapter XII. in the Chinese. The title in the first is "Reflection" (Appamada), in the second it is "Thoughtlessness" (Fang-yih). The version in the latter is as follows: "Obedience to Moral Law is the path of Immortality; thoughtlessness is the road (*king*) of death. Those who do not covet do not die, but those who lose reason (or, the way) are already dead.

"Those thoroughly wise guard the most excellent path of Reason (Religion), and in the end escape the results of thoughtlessness; freed from covetousness, they arrive at a condition of perfect joy, and from that advance to Nirvâna (the happiness of Bôdhi). Always jealous in guarding the way of Reason (Bôdhi), watchful over himself, careful in his conduct, the unwearied, obtains deliverance from the world, and arrives at the highest bliss. By right reflection and constant watchfulness, acting purely, overcoming the evil, binding himself to the precepts of the law—not offending in any of these things then his good name will increase. By exertion and banishing listlessness, by restraint and self-control, the wise man is able to make for himself an anchor-brightness (qu. the* brightness of the water flowing past the cable attached to an anchor), which no adverse tide can carry away."

It will be seen from this extract that there is a parallel vein of thought in both versions, although they differ in minor details; but not more widely than we should expect in translations made from copies found in countries so widely separated as China and Ceylon.

The work found in the same *Case*, and called *Fa-keu-pi-hu-king*, contains the Avadânas or stories connected with the verses of the Dhammapada; I am unable to say how far these agree with the Southern version of the same tales—they certainly differ *in toto* from the stories found in the Burmese Translation made by Captain Rogers *(Buddhaghosha's Parables)*; but yet there may be a connection with the more trustworthy Pali copy. The division of verses in this work is the same as in the former copy, and each verse has a tale appended to it. The third work, which bears the title "Chu'h-yau-king," is another copy of the Dhammapada in a thousand gâthas; it is evidently an expanded version of the original, and was not translated into Chinese until about 400 A.D.

The compilation of all these works is attributed to Bhadanta Dharmatrâta, who was the uncle of Vasumitra, and lived probably in the first century B.C.

The Sutra which is found in Case XVII., and named *Fuh* (for *Fo*)*-mieh-to-hau-kwan-hom-tsang-sang-king*, is one that deserves some notice, not only on account of its primitive character, but for the curious matter to which it relates, viz., the ancient mode of burial in use among the *Chakravartins*, or, universal monarchs. It is well known that Sakya Buddha directed his funeral obsequies to be conducted according to this rule, and it is a question of some importance who and what these Chakravartins were, and what was the character of their Sepulture. The following abstract of the Sutra in question may throw a little light on the matter. Bound up with this Sutra, and forming a component part of it, is the History of Buddha's begging-dish, or Patra; and there are such curious resemblances between this history and the Story of the Sangreal (the *Sacred dish*), that it is almost impossible not to recur to the Tale of Arthur and his *Round* Table, connected as it is with this Story of the Holy Dish and Sir Galahad, the pure knight.

"*Respecting the funeral rites of the body or relics of Buddha.*"

Thus have I heard. On a time the Blessed of the world (Bhagavat) was travelling through the country of the flowery people (Kusumapura). Then Ananda, bent on the advantage of men, asked him thus: "Bhagavat! after the Nirvâna, what is the character of the worship to be paid to the remains of the body of the Blessed one?" Bhagavat answered, "After my Nirvâna, my remains shall be reverently treated, according to the rules or customs of the pure-minded man (Brahmachari), whose life (family) is extinct." "And what are those rules?" enquired Ananda: to which the Blessed one replied, "According to the method of the flying, or, space-traversing, kings (Chakravartins), so shall my funeral obsequies be conducted." Again Ananda asked of what sort these were—to which Bhagavat replied, "At the time of the funeral of a Holy King, his body is swathed in a thousand folds of pure linen (napkins), and then sprinkled with perfumes and placed on a pyre of scented wood four-square, and then, having set fire to it, and the body being burned, the bones are collected, and placed in a golden vase filled with scented liquor. Then is taken a large stone tile (or, of a stone make a tile), three cubits long and of equal breadth, and one cubit thick; and this is supported evenly on the four corners by four upright pillars, and then in the very centre, underneath, is placed the golden vase (so filled). Then from the immediate middle point of this slab, is raised the *t'sah* (*i.e.*, the high pole which is supposed to surmount the Stûpa), and on this pole the customary hangings and ornaments are placed as offerings; after which heap up the earth and form a mound (pah) to which offerings of perfumes and other things (viands) may be made, but in as much greater proportion to me (than to others), as my accumulated merit through past ages has made me the most honorable amongst all the teachers and leaders of men. And

* This expression is obscure. It means, literally, 'Silver-brightness,' or "Ingot-brightness." It may possibly allude to the silver streak of light on the running stream—which is unaffected by the current.

whoever thus honors my remains, if it be only by helping with a handful of earth to raise a mound, or afterwards by offering to it, his merit shall be incalculable, and his present happiness and welfare equally great. Such is the law respecting my relics."

"Once more with respect to my alms-dish, the reverence (sacrifice) paid to this shall be the means of rescuing the world from a state of misery, and whilst it rests with men of producing a religious spirit; and then a Shaman, by the power of truth, shall be the means of converting the world and leading them back from error, so as to escape Hell, and attain to the three blissful conditions of Being."

Ananda asked what alms-dish Buddha spoke of.

"Even my own," Bhagavat replied, "which was given me by the four Maharâjas,—four being joined in one—the dish which I have ever used for collecting my food, whether it has been given or not.

"This dish, after my Nirvana, shall be a subject of contention among different countries, till the people having lapsed into disorder and wickedness, the duration of life shall be shortened, and general discontent and opposition to religion follow in consequence. Then the alms-dish shall appear in glory, shining forth with the five colors, and flying through the air—so it shall come and convert the people, and bring them back to obedience. It shall then go to the East and visit different countries, causing the people to obey the laws of religion, and giving increase and prosperity wherever it appears. But especially to the king of the farthest East shall the alms-dish be a token of happiness, and his life be agreeable to the same. After his death, the sins of impurity and lust shall prevail in every direction. The alms-dish being now dishonoured, the Nâgarâjas seeing it thus, shall take it to their own sea palace. to pay it reverence. And thus the existence of the alms-dish being forgotten, lo! every kind of sin and consequent misery will prevail, and the world becomes utterly degenerate. Then suddenly, a pure-minded man, but poor and needy, named Sse-Go, becoming a Bhikshu, and giving up all gluttony, wine-bibbing, and intercourse with women, shall come to the door of the Royal Palace and exclaim, "I know where the alms-dish is!" On this the king, overjoyed, shall ask him within and say, "Where is the alms-dish?" [On this follows a discourse, which is very obscure; but the main point is, that the alms-dish can only be recovered by one perfectly pure; and finally, the object is attained by this perfectly pure Shaman, and the earth recovered from its loss and degeneracy].

There are various Sutras relating to the Life of Buddha. Case XX. contains two; 1st. The "*Lalita Vistara*," under the Chinese title "*Fang-kwang-ta-chwang-yan-king*." As I have noticed in the Catalogue, this version corresponds accurately with that known to us through the translation of M. Foucaux. It dates in China from the Tang dynasty. The other translation, called "*Pou-yaou-king*," in the same Case, is of an earlier date, being in fact (according to M. Stas. Julien), the second version made in China of the Lalita Vistara. As I have observed in the Catalogue, M. Specht (quoted by M. Senart, *Legende du Bouddha*, p. 497. n. 4), has given us an accurate synopsis of the contents of this treatise. In Case XXXIV., there is the voluminous work termed *Fo-pen-hing-tsi-king*, which M. Wassilief identifies with the Abhinishkramana Sutra, and which I have partially translated as "A Romantic history of Sakya Buddha." In Case LXVI., is a work called "*Fo-pen-hing-king*," a title which might induce one to hope that it was the early copy of the Lalita Vistara, made by Chu-Fa-lan and others, in the year 72 A.D. But on examination, it proves to be a copy of the Buddha tcharitra, or, Life of Buddha, written in verse by Asvagosha Bodhisatwa, and translated into Chinese during the Sung dynasty.

Omitted from Case LXVIII. is an important Volume containing two short Sutras, both of them Memoirs of Buddha The first, *Siau-hing-pen-hi-king*, is an early life, translated into Chinese by Kong-mang-tsiang, A.D. 194; he was assisted in his work by a Shaman called Ta-lih of India (Chu); both these translators lived during the After Han dynasty. This book comprises seven sections, which are thus named. 1. Previous indications; this includes the prophecy of Dipankara, and the subsequent residence of Bodhisatwa in Heaven. 2. The Spiritual descent of Bodhisatwa to be incarnated. 3. Education and preparatory discipline [end of Part I]. 4. Excursions. 5. Leaving home. 6. Six years penance. 7. Conquest of Mâra.

This short Sutra is probably the most ancient memoir of Buddha extant in China and deserves especial attention. I shall only call attention to two singular features connected with it. First—in describing the incarnation of Buddha (Chap. 2), a phrase is used which I have not met with in any other Buddhist account of this event, viz., "*Shing-shin-kong-t'oi*," which is, literally translated, "The Holy Spirit descended into the womb;" and secondly, the name of Suddhôdana, the Father of Buddha, is constantly rendered *not* "tsing-fan," *i.e.*, "pure food;" but "tsing-pih," *i.e.*, "pure and white."

The second Sutra in this Volume is also an ancient life of Buddha, translated by an Upasikawa (lay disciple) belonging to the Getæ (yue-chi), during the Wu period, *circ* 170 A.D. It is called *Tai-tseu-sui-ying-pen-hi-king*, *i.e.*, the miraculous or glorious birth origin of the Great Son (Kumâra). It is not divided into chapters, but is in two parts and extends to the conversion of the Kasyâpas. It appears to be of a primitive character and deserves careful examination.

The Sutras belonging to the Great Development are so numerous and of such a scholastic character, that I should not be justified in offering any remarks upon them separately. As a whole they appear to be expansions of the primitive books, according to a systematic principle, and are comparatively uninteresting.*

Under the heading of Abhidharma, we find in the Catalogue nearly all the works known to us from the Nepalese sources. The wonderfully voluminous work in 600 Kiouen known as the Prajna Paramita Sutra (though really belonging to the Abhidharma class) was supposed to have been composed by Sariputra. The Chinese version was made by Hiouen Thsang, after four years incessant labor. This work will be found in the first 6 cases of the Catalogue. But the principal works of the Abhidharma class are in case L. and following Cases. It would be of great advantage to the Student of Buddhism if some of these intricate works were translated conjointly with their Sanscrit originals, of which there exist complete copies both in London and Cambrigde, as it is almost beyond the competency of any single scholar to undertake the translation of the Chinese Books without constant recourse to the Sanscrit.

The Miscellaneous.

Among the miscellaneous works in the Catalogue (a division which seems to agree with the Kshudaka of Csoma Korösi) may be mentioned the numerous Volumes containing Fables or Stories, such as e.gr. in Case LXVII., p. 88, the Satavadana, and on p. 89, No. 6, "various stories selected by Kumârajiva, or, in Case LXVI., p. 85, "The Sutra called the Treasury of Jewels," containing 121 Fables, and many others (particularly p. 89, *Ku-tsa-pi-u-king*); but, above all, the 120 Kiouen contained in Cases LXXII. and LXXIII., under the Title "*Fa-yuen-chu-lin*," or Pearls from the Garden of the Law—from which M. Stas. Julien translated the greater number of the Avadânas which he published under that name. [Under this head we may also refer to the work "*Chan-tsah-pe-un-king*," Case LXVI., p. 86.]

The numerous Encyclopædias and Catalogues (Vid. *Case XCI.*) will also attract the notice of the Student. These are the most valuable aids we have for a thorough appreciation of the part the Chinese have acted in the History of the Buddhist movement. Their accurate and exact Records of every Book introduced among them, its date and Translator's name, with a brief Memoir of the Translator appended, is of great service in gaining a knowledge of the way in which Buddhism gained its present position in the Empire, and is a proof of the care and accuracy with which events were chronicled.

The travels of the Pilgrims, Fa-Hian, and Hiouen Thsang, and others, need not be alluded to, but it would be perhaps of some service if the great work of Hiouen Thsang (the *Si-yu-ki*), were published in English, for general use.

The history of the Indian Patriarchs, and their work in India, is worth consideration, and perhaps, partial translation. At first sight, the records found in these books appear most valuable, but on further examination, the incidents found in them assume a fabulous character; but yet there are many allusions of historical importance.

There is a work in Case LXXVI., called "*Nan-hae-ki-kwei-chou'en*," which contains an interesting account of Buddhism in India and Ceylon, and is therefore deserving of especial notice. An analysis of this work would be very interesting.

It is worthy of notice that one of the earliest translators of Buddhist Books in China is known by the name of 'An, or, Ngan-shi-kao, belonging to the country called 'An-sik. Mr. Wylie considers 'An-sik as the counterpart of Arsak, or the Arsacidæ, or Parthians (Journal of the Anthropological Institute, Volume II., No. 3). The Chinese Buddhist records speak of 'An-shi-kao as the son of the king of these people, or the heir-apparent to the throne; but as he was converted to Buddhism, he gave up his royal title, and became a travelling mendicant or a missionary of the Buddhist religion, and reached as far as China. This is an interesting fact, as it shows what hold Buddhism had taken upon the Northern tribes, which afterwards exercised such an influence on the Western civilization.

Some of the translators also belonged to the tribe called "Yu-chi," generally considered as equivalent to Getæ (e.gr. Case XXXII., p. 39, letter *b*); but Mr. Wylie identifies these people with the 'Viddhals,' or 'Ephthalitæ' (White Huns), who acted such a conspicuous part in the history of the Byzantine Empire.

It is undoubtedly curious to know that these tribes, both Parthians and Huns, were at an early date influenced by Buddhist teaching; and it is probable, that in their migrations and subsequent intermixture with Western nations, they carried many of their ideas or legends with them, and this may account to a considerable extent for the prevalence of Buddhist modes of thought, and perhaps parallel lines of development in poetry and art, but especially architecture, to be found in the West.

I will conclude by drawing attention to the work *Kin-tsa-shi-lun*, Case LXV., which is said to have been composed by Kapila Rishi, and contains an account of the Sankhya philosophy. I would also mention that a work called *Shi-song-liu-pi-ni-tsu*, which has been placed, as it seems, by error in Case XV., contains a full account of the two first Buddhist Councils; the one consisting of 500 Rahats at Rajagriha, the other 110 years afterwards at Vaisali, called the Council of the 700. This work deserves further attention.